Barbecuing is more art than science,

with a little sport thrown in.

Theodore Andrew Witzel Sr.

Mary (Zuber) Witzel

Foreword

Gathering Around the Grill commemorates Onward Manufacturing Company's 100th Anniversary with a special collection of recipes using your barbecue. The twenty-one menus are designed for the many special occasions celebrated with friends and family. From Valentines Day to Christmas, last day of school to a picnic on the beach, a backyard skating party to a family reunion at the cottage, these pages show you the way to stress-free, enjoyable entertaining using the convenience of your grill. You will find that even in our Canadian climate, you can use your barbecue all year long. Whenever and wherever you gather with friends and family, the food that adds warmth to your occasion can be prepared outdoors as often as in.

With the combined experience from years of grilling, Andrea and Kris know how to get the best out of their barbecues and are adventurous when it comes to experimenting with recipes. In this book you will find some recipes that they have developed from unforgettable restaurant meals and their own versions of classics. Fresh, in-season foods, combined with staples from the pantry, are the foundation of all the recipes.

The menus Andrea and Kris put together for this book are tried and true meals that they have served at their own gatherings. The photographs are an album of special people in their lives enjoying the meals that these two women have prepared. The meals were so delicious and the parties so much fun that there was no need for food photography tricks that render the dishes inedible.

If you have an interest in grilling and entertaining, this cookbook will guide you through planning, organizing and sharing dozens of memorable meals.

Enjoy yourself!

Welcome Friends

Entertaining is a tradition that brings great enjoyment to our family. Learning early in our lives the joy that friendly gatherings bring grew from the roots of our mother, Mary (Zuber) Witzel. Her family was in the hospitality business for almost 70 years as proprietors of the Walper Hotel in Kitchener. When we were growing up our mother always welcomed our friends into our home at any time of day or night and took pleasure in preparing simple and special meals for any occasion.

This book is a celebration of our company's heritage and commemorates 100 years of dedication to our purpose of providing great products that our customers enjoy. Our valued associates, vendors and customers have all contributed immensely to our success. Yet with each new venture and exciting challenge, we have all kept in mind the importance of making time for family and friends.

Our grandfather, Theodore Adam Witzel began manufacturing fountain pens in Kitchener in 1904 when the city was still known as Berlin. Four years later, he founded Onward Manufacturing Company. It was the first company in Canada to make and sell vacuum sweepers and electric vacuum cleaners.

In 1936, our father, Theodore Andrew Witzel joined the company. With the onset of World War II, the business transformed from manufacturing vacuums to the production of military equipment in aid of the war effort. Shortly after the war, Onward resumed production of vacuum cleaners and hardware.

Today, we manufacture Broil King, Broil-Mate and Sterling gas barbecues in Canada and the USA and distribute our products throughout North America, Europe and many other countries. We also provide an array of barbecue tools and accessories under the brand names GrillPro and Barbecue Genius.

While the business has allowed us to enjoy friendships locally and around the world, it's those simple and special celebrations that have made our friendships memorable. So as you page through this cookbook created by my wife, Andrea and her good friend Kris, think about the memories you want to create when you invite your friends and family to enjoy these great recipes prepared on your barbecue.

Andrea has always been able to make me look good as a host and outdoor chef. And for that I am grateful. I am sure she and Kris will do the same for you.

On behalf of my brothers and our families, please enjoy.

Sincerely,

Gathering Around the Grill

Family and friends are a big part of our busy lives and we love to gather with them around our tables. With them we have celebrated many milestones and enjoyed countless meals, forging lifelong bonds and relationships.

We developed this twenty-one menu cookbook to inspire you to use your barbecue when celebrating special occasions. We know that grilling outdoors inherently brings a sense of casualness, comfort and relaxation to any gathering or occasion. Take the cooking outside, and the sounds, smells and sights evoke such anticipation that people can't resist being a part of it. And, of course, when the festivities wind down, everyone appreciates that clean-up is a breeze!

Our goal was to create manageable, healthy and delicious menus using the grill. Whatever your family's special occasions, you will find a seasonal menu in this book that will help inspire lasting memories. Simply by using the freshest foods possible, you have already created something special - strawberries in June, squash in the fall, asparagus in spring, blueberries in July. Root and cellared vegetables are staples during the months when the ground is frozen. And, yes, you can use your barbecue year round! During winter, dishes that require less attention, such as large roasts and poultry are a treat when prepared on the grill. Our warm weather menus let you enjoy the outdoors because almost everything is cooked outside.

Embrace the thought of hosting a party. Plan ahead, have fun, be creative, be resourceful. We hope this collection inspires you to create memorable occasions as you gather around the grill.

Andrea Witzel   *Kris Schumacher*

recipes and styling

Andrea Witzel & Kris Schumacher

photography

Bryn Gladding

design

Bravada Consumer Communications Inc.

How to use this book

MENUS

You will find menus in this book that are ideal for any season and the many special events throughout the year. The recipes are designed to serve 8 people; which makes them practical for an average sized dinner party. You can easily accommodate any number of guests by scaling the quantities up or down.

In each chapter, a section titled "Getting Organized," will help you with the advanced preparation. Following our tips for make-ahead items eases the pressure, allowing you more time to enjoy your own party. You will notice that not every recipe uses a barbecue. We have found that it is nice to have the option of using stovetops and ovens as well as the grill particularly when cooking for a crowd.

We have put these menus together because they have worked for parties with our families and friends. You are encouraged to pick and choose from these menus, recipes that you like and think would work best for your gathering. Some recipes may look daunting, but with practice they will become second nature. One of the secrets to successful entertaining is mastering a few sure-fire favourites. When they become your specialty, guests will eagerly anticipate an invitation.

HANDLE FOOD SAFELY

- Always thoroughly clean all surfaces, utensils, and kitchenware that have come into contact with raw meat

- After placing raw food on the grill, clean the utensils before using them on cooked food

- Use separate cutting boards for raw and ready foods

- The maximum time roasts should be left at room temperature is 1 hour; steaks, chops, chicken and fish, ½ hour

- Incorporate used marinades into sauces only after boiling the marinade for 5 minutes to kill accumulated bacteria

- Always use a meat thermometer to determine internal temperature, remembering that this temperature will continue to rise as the meat rests

- The thermometer is especially critical when using ground meats

HOW TO SHOP FOR YOUR INGREDIENTS

Getting organized includes shopping ahead. Visit your local farmers' markets for the freshest, local, in-season ingredients. Local can mean different things for different ingredients. It can mean buying within your region for meat, cheese and produce. It could mean choosing fish delivered from your closest seaport. It can also mean selecting specialty foods from different parts of our country.

Some classic pantry items such as olive oil and coconut milk cannot be sourced locally; however, they are mainstays of many dishes and are important to add to your pantry.

THE PANTRY

Keeping your pantry stocked with frequently used ingredients makes spontaneous entertaining much easier. Always use the best quality ingredients such as oils and vinegars as their excellence will shine through in your meals. Here are a few things to always have on hand for marinades, rubs, sauces, and vinaigrettes which quickly make simple foods interesting.

Oils	• olive, vegetable, sesame, avocado
Vinegars	• balsamic, rice, cider, red and white wine, tarragon
Sauces	• Worcestershire, soy, asian chili, sambal oelek, Dijon mustard, fish sauce
Sweeteners	• honey, maple syrup, brown and white sugar
Fruits/juices	• lemons, limes, oranges, canned coconut milk
Spirits	• beer, wine, Grand Marnier, sherry
Flavour boosters	• garlic, onions, shallots, ginger, chipotle chilis, fresh herbs
Seasonings	• dried herbs and spices such as salt, kosher salt, black pepper, cayenne pepper, paprika, chili powder, cumin, coriander, thyme, basil, oregano and cinnamon

THE TOOLS

The right tools are essential. Keep them handy, as they will make preparation easier.

Steel barbecue brush	• very important for keeping grids clean so you don't taste Tuesday's fish on Wednesday's pineapple
Long-handled tongs Long-handled spatula Silicone oven mitts	• help to keep your distance from the heat
Meat thermometer	• essential for ensuring that meat is cooked to your liking, and in the case of ground meat, to a safe standard
Cutting boards	• handy for carrying and carving • keep separate boards for raw and cooked foods
Silicone basting brushes Oil vapourizer	• useful for oiling your grids and food which is a must to prevent food from sticking
Aluminum drip pans	• good for catching drippings and containing liquids when using indirect and rotisserie cooking • keep the heat moist

THE ACCESSORIES

These accessories can enhance your cooking experience.

Rotisserie	• best for boneless roasts, chickens, or for rotisserie baskets • constant turning keeps food very moist
Side burner	• helps to prepare the whole meal in one spot • cooks side dishes, reheats marinades
Pizza stone	• protects dough from scorching • retains heat for crispy crust
Grill basket	• makes turning over easy eg. delicate fish
Wok topper Grill topper	• use for stir-frying vegetables or smaller morsels, such as shrimp
Griddle	• takes breakfast outside to cook bacon, eggs and pancakes
Cedar planks	• add smoky flavour to fish, chicken, pork and even fruit
Chicken roaster	• simplifies the cooking of beer can chicken (*p. 121*) as it includes the drip pan
Bamboo or Stainless steel skewers	• allow you to combine morsels of different foods in interesting ways

TEMPERATURE GUIDE

Cooking in the great outdoors can present some challenges and variability. Our recipes outline cooking times and temperatures assuming a moderate climate without winds. Once you get to know your grill (size and models will vary) in your climate, you can learn to adjust to them. Some of the factors within your control for more consistent results are:

- Grids: The use of cast iron grids will retain more heat.
- Location: Position your grill in a place that is away from direct prevailing winds.
- Temperature: Bring foods to room temperature before grilling and use the upper racks for less intense heat.
- Equipment: Your barbecue should be equipped with a temperature gauge in the lid and fully adjustable controls.
- Spacing: Allow for spacing between foods so that air can circulate and prevent slower cooking time.
- Lid position: Keep the lid closed where possible. To reduce heat when cooking on low with the lid closed, turn the middle burners off. If grilling with the lid open, we recommend that you preheat the barbecue on medium and adjust the settings to medium high.

TEMPERATURE AT GRID LEVEL

TEMPERATURE SETTINGS	HIGH	MEDIUM	LOW
Lid Closed		650 - 750°F	450 - 550°F
Lid Open	600 - 750°F	450 - 550°F	300 - 400°F

Note: Pressure delivered to the house varies and pressure loss varies as it is delivered to the appliance. It is normal for a Natural Gas barbecue to operate 100 °F cooler than a Liquid Propane barbecue due to varying delivery pressure and pressure loss through the supply lines. Use slightly higher settings for Natural Gas.

Barbecue cooking methods

There are several different methods of cooking on the barbecue: direct grilling, indirect cooking, rotisserie cooking, plank grilling, smoking and slow roasting. The method used is determined by the cut of meat or the type of food you are cooking. It is possible to cook a variety of foods at the same time using different grilling methods; however, setting up your barbecue correctly is critical. In this section we outline the three main methods: direct, indirect and rotisserie cooking. The Cedar Plank Salmon recipe on page 67, provides detailed instructions for grilling with a cedar plank.

DIRECT GRILLING

The direct grilling method involves cooking the food on grids directly over the lit burners. We recommend direct grilling for most quick-cooking foods such as steaks, chops, fish, burgers, kebabs and vegetables, as well as breads, fruit and desserts. In the sections that follow you will find more detailed instructions for using the direct method for grilling steak, other meats, fish and vegetables. We have also included step-by-step instructions for creating "Perfect Grill Marks" on meat and vegetables using this method.

Marinades, rubs and sauces can be used when direct grilling to create interesting dishes full of flavour. Marinades can also be used to create a barrier from intense heat, to tenderize less tender cuts of meat and to increase their juiciness. Always apply sugary sauces at the very end of the cooking time to prevent scorching.

GRILL SET-UP

- preheat the grill on MEDIUM for 10 minutes
- clean the cooking grids with a wire grill brush
- spray or brush on vegetable oil with a basting brush to prevent food from sticking
- adjust the heat setting before placing food on the grids by following our meat and vegetable grilling guides

PERFECT GRILL MARKS

When you want the best presentation for your grilled foods, follow this guide.

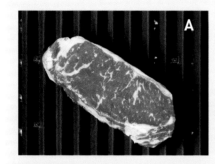  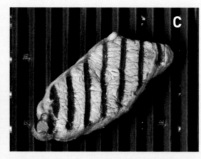 

Brush grids with vegetable or olive oil and set to cooking temperature. Place food on the barbecue at a 45° angle and cook according to the timing on the grilling charts that follow.

Turn the food over, grilling on the same 45° angle.

Turn the food over and grill on the opposite 45° angle.

Finally turn the food over and grill on the same 45° angle.

DIRECT GRILLING PERFECT STEAKS

Steak remains everyone's absolute favourite meat on the barbecue, so use the following guide to make it perfect every time. For best results, use tender cuts of the best quality meat. We prefer new york strips, filet mignon, rib-eye, and porterhouse or t-bone. For less tender cuts such as flank, hanger and blade, marinate the meat for at least 4 hours to tenderize it. Then grill it with the same timing and carve it thinly against the grain.

Meat Thickness			Heat Setting	Minutes Per Side for Perfect Grill Marks				Total Time
1 ½"	1"	¾"		A	B	C	D	
		RARE	MEDIUM/HIGH	1 ½	1 ½	1 ½	1 ½	6 min.
	RARE	MEDIUM/RARE	MEDIUM/HIGH	1 ¾	1 ¾	1 ¾	1 ¾	7 min.
RARE	MEDIUM/RARE	MEDIUM	MEDIUM/HIGH	2	2	2	2	8 min.
MEDIUM/RARE	MEDIUM	WELL	MEDIUM/HIGH	2 ½	2 ½	2 ½	2 ½	10 min.
MEDIUM	WELL		MEDIUM	3	3	3	3	12 min.
WELL			MEDIUM	4	4	4	4	16 min.

Note: Bone-in cuts take slightly longer to grill.

DIRECT GRILLING OTHER MEATS

Listed below are suggested times for cooking some other popular small cuts of meat:

Cut of Meat	Heat	Minutes Per Side for Perfect Grill Marks				Total Time	Comments
		A	B	C	D		
Hamburgers	MEDIUM	2 ½	2 ½	2 ½	2 ½	10 min.	Cook to internal temp of 160°F/71°C
Lamb Chops (1" medium)	MEDIUM	2 ½	2 ½	2 ½	2 ½	10 min.	Sear chops on each side to preserve juiciness
Pork Chops (1")	MEDIUM/LOW	2 ½	2 ½	2 ½	2 ½	10 min.	Cook until golden brown outside and juices run clear
Boneless Chicken Breast	MEDIUM/LOW	3	3	3	3	12 min.	Brush with sauce or glaze after the last turn
Bone-in Chicken Breast	MEDIUM/LOW	5-6	5-6	5-6	5-6	20-25 min.	Sear the chicken, skin side down, then reduce heat and cook until tender and cooked through, continuing to turn the chicken
Sausage	MEDIUM/LOW	6	6	6	6	24 min.	Cook thoroughly until no longer pink inside
Rack of Lamb	MEDIUM	5-6	5-6	5-6	5-6	20-25 min.	See *page 162* for a delicious recipe
Skewers: (chicken, pork)	MEDIUM	2 ½	2 ½	2 ½	2 ½	10 min.	Soak wooden skewers ½ hour before using
Skewers: (beef, lamb)	MEDIUM	2	2	2	2	8 min.	

DIRECT GRILLING FISH AND SEAFOOD

Some firm-fleshed fish steaks like swordfish, tuna, salmon and halibut can be cooked with Perfect Grill Marks.

Fish Steaks	Heat	Minutes Per Side for Perfect Grill Marks				Total Time
		A	B	C	D	
1 inch thick (rare)	MEDIUM/HIGH	1 ½	1 ½	1 ½	1 ½	6 min.
1 inch thick (medium)	MEDIUM/HIGH	2	2	2	2	8 min.

To cook fillet of salmon, place skin side down on a hot grill for 2 min. at MEDIUM/HIGH. Slip the spatula between the skin and the fish. Turn onto a well-oiled grill at a 45° angle for 1½ min. at MEDIUM. Rotate the fish 90° and grill 1½ min. on MEDIUM. Serve with grill marks-up for perfect presentation.

Fillet of Salmon	Heat	Minutes Per Side for Perfect Grill Marks			Total Time
		A	B	C	
1 inch thick (rare)	MEDIUM/HIGH, then MEDIUM	2	1 ½	1 ½	5 min.
1 inch thick (medium)	MEDIUM/HIGH, then MEDIUM	2	2	2	6 min.

More delicate fish like pickerel, bass, perch, tilapia, or trout are best cooked using one of the following 4 methods:

- In a well-oiled fish basket.
- In a cast-iron pan on the side-burner.
- On well-oiled grids.
- On a cedar plank: See our recipe for Cedar Plank Salmon for detailed directions (page 67).

As a general rule, cook fish ten minutes for each inch of thickness using any of the first three methods. Cooking on a plank requires more time.

Seafood	Heat	Total Time	Comments
Shrimp (medium or large)	MEDIUM	4-6 min.	It can be helpful to use a wok topper. Cook just until pink and opaque. Do not overcook.
Mussels	MEDIUM	5-6 min.	Scrub well. Discard any open raw mussels. After cooking, discard any closed mussels.
Scallops	MEDIUM	4-6 min.	Turn once halfway through.
Lobster	MEDIUM	8-10 min.	Thaw if frozen. Grill shell side down, brushing with butter and lemon juice. Cook until opaque and separating from shell.

DIRECT GRILLING VEGETABLES

Grilling adds a smoky, delicious dimension to most vegetables. We always grill extra so that we can use leftovers in soups, salads, sandwiches and on pizzas and pasta. If the vegetables have a large surface area, use the technique for Perfect Grill Marks.

Vegetable	Preparation	Approximate Cooking Time
Asparagus	Wash and snap off ends. Drizzle with olive oil and sprinkle with kosher salt before cooking.	Grill on MEDIUM/LOW 6-8 minutes, turning once.
Baked Potatoes	Scrub well and poke with sharp knife in several places. Wrap well in foil and place on upper rack.	Cook on MEDIUM 35-45 minutes.
Beets	Scrub well. Drizzle with olive oil and sprinkle with salt and pepper. Wrap in foil with a sprig of fresh thyme.	Grill on MEDIUM for one hour on upper rack, until tender.
Cauliflower	Cut into medium sized flowerets. Spread on a cookie sheet, drizzle with olive oil, and sprinkle with salt and pepper.	Roast on the upper rack for 25 minutes, turning frequently until golden brown.
Corn on the Cob	Do not husk, but remove top silk, and soak in cold water for 20 minutes, shake off water.	Cook 20 minutes on MEDIUM/LOW, carefully pull back husks and serve with butter, salt and pepper.
Eggplant	Peel if desired, and slice lengthwise or crosswise. Sprinkle sliced eggplant with salt, and let drain 20 minutes on paper towels to remove any bitterness. Wipe off excess salt and moisture, and brush liberally with olive oil.	Grill a total of 10-12 minutes, following directions for Perfect Grill Marks (page 15).
Grilled Peppers	Wash and cut into large chunks. Remove ribs and seeds. Drizzle with olive oil.	Grill on MEDIUM/LOW for a total of 10-12 minutes, following directions for Perfect Grill Marks (page 15).
Mushrooms	Wipe clean with cloth or paper towel. Remove any woody stems. Toss with seasoned olive oil or vinaigrette to marinate.	Grill on MEDIUM/LOW 5-7 minutes.
Baby & Fingerling Potatoes	Scrub well. Toss with olive oil and kosher salt.	Grill on MEDIUM 25-30 minutes turning often.
Onions	Cut into thick slices. Push a skewer through sideways to hold intact, and brush with olive oil.	Grill 20-30 minutes on upper rack on MEDIUM/LOW, following directions for Perfect Grill Marks. If desired, wrap in foil at this point and continue cooking until caramelized.
Roasted garlic	Cut top off whole garlic head. Drizzle with olive oil, wrap in foil, and place on upper rack.	Grill on LOW 30 minutes.
Roasted Peppers	Wash and place on the grill whole.	Grill on MEDIUM until skin is charred all over. Once cooked, place in a paper bag to steam skin loose. When cool enough to handle, peel and remove seeds.
Sweet Potatoes, sliced	Peel and cut into slices lengthwise. Brush with garlic and rosemary infused olive oil.	Grill on MEDIUM/LOW for a total of 20 minutes, following the directions for Perfect Grill Marks (page 15).

Vegetable	Preparation	Approximate Cooking Time
Sweet Potatoes, whole	Scrub well, poke with a sharp knife and wrap in foil. Place on upper rack of barbecue.	Grill on MEDIUM 35-40 minutes.
Tomatoes	Wash and cut in half. Loosen and remove seeds, then sprinkle with salt and drain on paper towels for 10 minutes to drain. Rub with cut garlic, and drizzle with olive oil.	Grill on LOW for a total of 15-20 minutes, following directions for Perfect Grill Marks (page 15).
Zucchini	Slice lengthwise or crosswise as preferred. Drizzle with olive oil and salt.	Grill on MEDIUM/LOW for a total of 8 minutes, following the directions for Perfect Grill Marks (page 15).

ROTISSERIE COOKING

Constant turning of the meat while rotisserie cooking allows it to self-baste with natural juices, resulting in exceptionally moist and tender roasts. The best cuts of meat for rotisserie cooking are tightly tied, boned or boneless cuts; however, you can use cuts with the bone in if you carefully balance them on the spit so they turn easily.

Your barbecue may be equipped with a rear rotisserie burner or you may use the lower burners. We have outlined the grill set-up for both kinds of rotisserie cooking below. It may be possible to set up your barbecue to rotisserie meat at the same time as you grill other foods. Simply set the meat on one side of the rotisserie and leave the racks in place on the opposite side of the grill.

USING THE REAR ROTISSERIE BURNER

ARRANGING THE GRILL

- remove cooking grids and warming racks from barbecue if necessary
- centre a drip pan under the rotisserie positioning it so it will be beneath the centre of the roast
- preheat the barbecue with rotisserie burner on MEDIUM HIGH for 10 minutes

PLACING THE MEAT ON THE SPIT ROD

- slide one of the skewer forks onto the rod and tighten it securely
- insert the spit rod lengthwise into the centre of the roast securing it in place with the remaining fork
- tighten the fork securely

TESTING THAT THE MEAT IS EVENLY BALANCED ON THE SPIT

- loosen the spit balance
- lay the rod over the sink, allowing the heavier side of the roast to rotate to the bottom
- adjust the balance to the highest point to counterbalance the weight, and tighten the rod handle
- insert the spit rod into the rotisserie motor and turn rotisserie motor on
- check to see if the meat turns smoothly while cooking and adjust the balance as necessary

USING THE ROTISSERIE WITH THE MAIN BURNERS

ARRANGING THE GRILL

- remove cooking grids and warming racks from barbecue
- centre a drip pan under the rotisserie, positioning it so it will be beneath the center of the roast
- fill the drip pan to 1" from the top with water, wine or juice and any herbs that might complement the flavours
- preheat the barbecue on MEDIUM for 10 minutes

PLACING THE MEAT ON THE SPIT ROD

- slide one of the skewer forks onto the rod and tighten it securely
- insert the spit rod lengthwise into the centre of the roast securing it in place with the remaining fork
- tighten the fork securely

TESTING THAT THE MEAT IS EVENLY BALANCED ON THE SPIT

- loosen the spit balance
- lay the rod over the sink, allowing the heavier side of the roast to rotate to the bottom
- adjust the balancer to the highest point to counterbalance the weight, and tighten the rod handle
- insert the spit rod into the rotisserie motor and turn it on
- check to see if the meat turns smoothly while cooking and adjust the balancer as necessary

Note: Never let the drip pan run dry as it may cause a flash fire. Keep a pitcher of hot water handy and when the water is running low, carefully refill the drip pan with hot water, using an oven mitt to protect your hand from steam burns.

INDIRECT COOKING

The indirect method of cooking is a slower cooking technique for larger cuts of meat such as roasts or poultry. As the name implies, the food is not grilled directly over the heat, but by hot air circulating around the food. There are two indirect methods: the drip pan method and the unlit burner method. Both rely on lower heat settings with the lid of the barbecue closed. With no need to turn or baste the roast, the result is worry-free barbecuing with little chance of flare-ups.

SET-UP FOR THE DRIP PAN METHOD

- remove grids and, if necessary, the warming racks
- place the drip pan beneath the center of the meat to be barbecued

Note: Depending on the other menu items, and on the size of your barbecue, you may want to position the roast to one side, allowing you to prepare other dishes at the same time.

- pour water and other cooking liquid into the drip pan

Note: Fruit juices, such as lemon, orange, pineapple, cranberry or apple, and red or white wine add delicious flavours.

- replace the cooking grids
- preheat the barbecue on MEDIUM for 10 minutes
- adjust heat to MEDIUM or MEDIUM/LOW
- spray or brush the cooking grids with vegetable oil to prevent food from sticking
- place the meat directly on the grids above the drip pan
- close the barbecue lid

Note: Always cook with the lid closed. The juices and drippings will fall and mix with the contents of the drip pan. The mixture heats up and vapourizes, automatically basting the food.

Never let the drip pan run dry! As the mixture in the drip pan heats up it will result in a diminished amount of liquid in the pan. Check the drip pan often and use a pitcher or baster to carefully pour in more warm liquid. During the cooking process, fat will drip from the meat. If the drip pan is dry, the fat will superheat and catch fire. Should this occur, turn off the burners, open the lid and extinguish the fire with baking soda. Do not use water to try to put out the fire.

SET-UP FOR ONE-BURNER METHOD

- remove grids, and if necessary, the warming racks
- place a drip pan on the side of the barbecue where the meat will be cooked
- return the grids to the barbecue
- preheat the barbecue on MEDIUM for 10 minutes
- turn off the burners on one side of the barbecue
- brush or spray cooking grids with vegetable oil
- sear the meat on all sides using the lit side of the barbecue
- transfer the meat over to the unlit side, centred over the drip pan
- regulate the heat setting to maintain desired temperature

Note: Always use a meat thermometer to ensure that the food is cooked to the desired degree of doneness for maximum juiciness and tenderness. Place the tip of the thermometer into the centre of the meat, away from bones and fat. Please refer to the cooking guide on page 17 for recommended cooking times and internal temperatures. We generally recommend cooking at a MEDIUM/LOW heat setting when using this method.

COOKING TIMES FOR ROASTS

These times are approximate and may vary with the thickness of the roast, and the internal temperature of the food before cooking. For best results, bring meat close to room temperature before placing on the barbecue. A longer, thinner roast will cook more quickly than a thick roast of the same weight.

Cut of Meat	Heat Control Setting	Approximate Cooking Time	Internal Cooking Temperature
BEEF			
Rare	MEDIUM-MEDIUM/LOW	18-20 min./lb	130°F/55°C
Medium Rare	MEDIUM-MEDIUM/LOW	20-22 min./lb	140°F/60°C
Medium	MEDIUM-MEDIUM/LOW	22-25 min./lb	150°F/66°C
Well Done	MEDIUM-MEDIUM/LOW	25-30 min./lb	160°F/71°C
PORK			
Medium	MEDIUM-MEDIUM/LOW	20-25 min./lb	160°F/71°C
Well Done	MEDIUM-MEDIUM/LOW	25-30 min./lb	170°F/77°C
LAMB			
Rare	MEDIUM-MEDIUM/LOW	18-20 min./lb	135°F/57°C
Medium	MEDIUM-MEDIUM/LOW	20-25 min./lb	145°F/63°C
POULTRY			
Whole Chicken	MEDIUM-MEDIUM/LOW	18-20 min./lb	180°F/83°C (dark meat)
Whole Turkey	MEDIUM-MEDIUM/LOW	18-20 min./lb	170°F/77°C (breast meat)

If using the rear rotisserie burner, heat control settings may need to be slightly higher.

awaken your senses...

Jewel Cocktails

•

Thai Chicken Patties
with Spicy Dipping Sauce

•

Grilled Asparagus and
Prosciutto Spears

•

Avocado and Arugula Salad

•

Honey Garlic Leg of Lamb
on the Rotisserie

•

Moroccan Couscous

•

Stir-Fried Vegetables

•

Rhubarb Pudding Cake

Serves 8

Spring gets you energized with the first signs of colour in your garden. With all of the fresh flavours of the season available, you will enjoy creating this refreshing menu highlighting rhubarb, spring lamb and asparagus.
This dinner is perfect for any number of spring occasions: Mothers' Day, homecoming for university students, Easter, or a special birthday. Your guests will warm to this distinctive blend of exotic and familiar flavours.

Getting Organized

Up to one week ahead:
Make and freeze chicken patties to have on hand.

One day ahead:
Marinate lamb, make couscous, and prepare vinaigrette, stir-fry sauce and dipping sauce.

The morning of:
Prepare the vegetables for the stir-fry, and make the rhubarb pudding cakes.

As the night unfolds:
Grill the asparagus and the chicken patties.
Prepare lamb for the rotisserie and start grilling 1½ hours before serving time.

Immediately before serving:
Stir-fry the vegetables.

Jewel Cocktails

	Juice of ½ a lime		
2½ oz	vodka	¼ oz	cassis
2½ oz	cherry juice	¼ oz	Cointreau
		1	bottle chilled Prosecco

In a cocktail shaker, combine lime juice, vodka, cherry juice, cassis and Cointreau. Shake with ice and strain into martini glasses. Top with a splash of Prosecco.

Thai Chicken Patties with Spicy Dipping Sauce

1½ lbs	lean ground chicken	½ cup	fresh cilantro, finely chopped
1	8 oz can waterchestnuts, rinsed and drained	1¼ tsp	kosher salt
1 bunch	scallions, chopped	1	egg white, lightly beaten
1	jalapeno pepper, minced		vegetable oil

Place chicken in a large bowl and set aside. Place the water chestnuts, scallions and jalapeno pepper into the food processor and pulse until finely chopped. Toss the water chestnut mixture into the bowl with the chicken, add cilantro, salt and egg white and gently mix together with your hands until just combined.

Line a cookie sheet or other flat-bottomed dish that will fit in your freezer with parchment paper. Using a spoon and moistened hand, form the mixture into small, bite-sized patties, and lay them on the prepared sheet, adding more layers of parchment paper as necessary. Dipping the spoon in water and continuing to moisten your fingers will help prevent sticking.

Place the tray in the freezer until patties are frozen solid. Peel the chicken patties off the parchment and store them in plastic freezer bags or other airtight container until ready to cook.

Preheat barbecue and reduce temperature to MEDIUM/LOW. Brush or spray both the chicken patties and the grill liberally with vegetable oil to prevent sticking. Grill from frozen until cooked through, about 10 minutes, turning to create Perfect Grill Marks (page 15).

SPICY DIPPING SAUCE:

⅓ cup	rice vinegar	2 cloves	garlic, finely minced
⅓ cup	Asian fish sauce	2 tbsp	soy sauce
⅓ cup	fresh lime juice	1½ tsp	Asian chili paste
1 tbsp	packed brown sugar	¼ cup	packed fresh mint leaves, chopped
3 tbsp	water	2 tbsp	finely shredded peeled carrot

Mix all ingredients in a small glass bowl.

Grilled Asparagus and Prosciutto Spears

2 lbs	asparagus, cleaned well
1 tbsp	olive oil
12-15	slices prosciutto

2 tbsp	balsamic vinegar
	Salt and freshly cracked black pepper

Preheat barbecue on MEDIUM for 10 minutes. Meanwhile, prepare asparagus by rinsing thoroughly in cold water to remove sand. Snap off the woody ends. Toss lightly in olive oil, place on grill and cook for 8 minutes, turning once. Remove from grill and sprinkle lightly with salt.

Meanwhile, cut each piece of prosciutto in half, lengthwise. Wrap bottom half of each spear of asparagus in prosciutto. Arrange on platter and sprinkle with balsamic vinegar and freshly cracked black pepper.

Avocado and Arugula Salad

Avocado oil adds a rich flavour. You may substitute with olive or canola oil.

For the Vinaigrette:

2 tbsp	cilantro, finely chopped
½ tsp	ground cumin
1 tsp	brown sugar
	pinch kosher salt
	a few grinds black pepper
1 tbsp	cider vinegar

1 tbsp	fresh lime juice
¼ cup	avocado oil, or olive oil
8 cups	arugula, torn
1 cup	cherry tomatoes
½	red onion, thinly sliced
2	ripe avocados, cut into chunks

Whisk together the first 7 ingredients in a large salad bowl. Slowly drizzle in avocado oil while continuing to whisk. Just before serving, cut the avocado and toss with arugula, cherry tomatoes, onions and dressing.

Honey Garlic Leg of Lamb on the Rotisserie

2	3½ lb boneless leg of lamb		juice and zest of 1 lemon
2 tbsp	lemon pepper		juice and zest of 1 orange
¼ cup	butter	⅓ cup	honey
2 tsp	dried rosemary		*For the Drip Pan*:
3 cloves	garlic, minced		optional, 2 sprigs fresh rosemary

Up to 24 hours or at least 1 hour ahead of cooking, rub the meat all over with lemon pepper. Melt the butter in the microwave, and stir in the remaining ingredients, except for the honey. Place the lamb in a heavy resealable plastic bag, pour the marinade over, seal and refrigerate. One hour before cooking, remove lamb from refrigerator to bring it close to room temperature. Remove from marinade, pat dry with paper towels, and brush lightly with olive oil. Reserve marinade.

Refer to page 23 for set up directions on rotisserie cooking. If using the main burners, the addition of wine or fruit juice and a sprig or two of fresh rosemary adds nice flavour too.

Preheat the barbecue on MEDIUM. Meanwhile, skewer the meat on the rotisserie rod. Tie meat tightly and fasten securely with the prongs. Position the counterbalance for even rotation. To do this, lay the rod with meat over the kitchen sink allowing the heaviest side of the roast to turn to the bottom. With the counterbalance loosened, rotate it to the opposite side, facing up. Twist the end of the spit rod to secure tightly. If using main burners, reduce temperature to MEDIUM/LOW. If using rear rotisserie burner only, reduce the temperature to MEDIUM. Place the spit rod on the barbecue, inserting into the motor and close the lid. Check the water level in the drip pan every 20 minutes to ½ hour to ensure that the liquid has not evaporated. Carefully pour in additional HOT water as needed, using oven mitts to protect your hands.

For best results, use a meat thermometer to ensure that the lamb is cooked to your liking (Rare 135ºF, Medium 145ºF), but, as a general guide, aim for 20 minutes per pound for medium doneness. Place on a carving board, tent with foil, and cover with a kitchen towel to rest and reabsorb juices. Meanwhile, pour reserved marinade into a small saucepan and add honey. Bring to a boil, then simmer until slightly thickened, for at least 5 minutes. Slice lamb and serve with the reheated marinade.

Moroccan Couscous

2 tsp	canola oil	1 tsp	cumin, ground
1	onion, diced	1 tsp	chili pepper flakes
2 garlic	cloves, minced	½ tsp	salt
1 tsp	fresh ginger, minced	1	medium zucchini, diced
3 cups	chicken stock	½ cup	currants
2	large carrots, diced	1½ cups	medium grain couscous
1 tsp	black pepper, freshly ground	½ cup	fresh parsley, chopped
1 tsp	coriander, ground		

Heat oil over medium heat and add onion, garlic and ginger. Saute for 2 minutes, until softened. Add chicken stock, carrots, black pepper, coriander, cumin, chili pepper flakes and salt. Cover and bring to a boil. Reduce heat and simmer 5 - 7 minutes. Add zucchini and cook 2 - 3 minutes longer. Stir in currants.

In a large bowl, combine couscous with chicken stock and vegetable mixture. Cover and let stand for 5 minutes. Fluff, taste and adjust seasonings. Garnish with parsley, just before serving.

Stir-Fried Vegetables

2 cups	broccoli, cut into small florets		1 tsp	asian chili sauce
2 cups	cauliflower, cut into small florets		1 tbsp	lime juice
1	red bell pepper, cut into 1-inch pieces		1 tbsp	oyster sauce
1	zucchini, sliced 1/4" thick		1 tbsp	honey
1 cup	carrots, sliced on the diagonal		1 clove	garlic, pressed
1 cup	sugar snap peas, strings removed		1 tbsp	fresh ginger, grated
3	green onions, sliced sharply on the diagonal		1 tsp	kosher salt

For the Marinade:

For the Garnish:

2 tbsp	canola oil		2 tbsp	fresh cilantro, chopped
1 tbsp	sesame oil		2 tbsp	toasted sesame seeds

Prepare all the vegetables and place in a large bowl. In a small bowl, whisk together the marinade ingredients. Pour the marinade over the vegetables and toss to coat evenly. Preheat barbecue on MEDIUM, placing a Wok Topper or Grill Topper on the cooking grids. When it is nice and hot, brush or spray the wok liberally with vegetable oil.

Place all the vegetables into the wok, and stir briefly, then close the barbecue lid. Continue to toss the vegetables with tongs until they are tender-crisp and starting to brown, about 10 minutes.

Using good quality oven mitts, transfer the vegetables to a heated serving platter, and sprinkle with chopped cilantro and toasted sesame seeds.

Rhubarb Pudding Cake

3 cups	fresh rhubarb, chopped in ½" pieces			pinch salt
3 tbsp	butter, softened		½ cup	milk
1¼ cups	sugar, divided		½ cup	orange juice
¾ cup	unbleached flour		1 tbsp	cornstarch
1 tsp	baking powder		1 tsp	orange zest
½ tsp	cinnamon			
½ tsp	ground ginger			
¼ tsp	nutmeg, freshly ground			

optional garnish:
candied ginger and toasted pumpkin seeds

Preheat oven to 350ºF. Spread the prepared rhubarb in a greased 8" square pan, or in 8 small greased ramekins.

Cream together the butter and ¾ cup sugar.

Combine the flour, baking powder, spices and salt. Add these dry ingredients to the butter mixture alternating with the milk, in three additions. Mix until just combined, and spread this batter over the rhubarb.

Heat orange juice in the microwave or in a saucepan. Add the remaining ½ cup sugar, cornstarch, and orange zest. Pour evenly over the batter.

Bake 45 minutes to an hour or until the top is golden and crusty, or 40-45 minutes for individual servings.

Optional: Sprinkle with chopped candied ginger and toasted pumpkin seeds when fully baked. Serve with Vanilla Ice Cream.

coming of age...

34

Warm Shrimp Cocktail

•

Prime Rib of Beef with
Béarnaise Sauce

•

Zucchini Rolls

•

Grilled Tomatoes

•

Grilled Baby Potatoes

•

Grilled Pound Cake with
Grilled Fruit & Chocolate Sauce

Serves 8

Graduation ushers in a new beginning. Celebrate this milestone with a sophisticated menu that reflects this joyful step into adulthood by serving something extraordinary from the grill. Start with warm shrimp cocktail, carve the grilled prime rib and conclude the meal with grilled pound cake and fruit drizzled with chocolate sauce. This menu has lots of opportunity for make-ahead preparation. If you love to bake, try our favourite pound cake recipe and chocolate sauce. If not, store-bought substitutes will grill up nicely and nobody will know the difference!

GETTING ORGANIZED

Up to one week ahead:
Bake and freeze the pound cake, and prepare the chocolate sauce.

Up to one day ahead:
Make the cocktail sauce for the shrimp and prepare the zucchini rolls.

The morning of:
Prepare the prime rib, tomatoes and potatoes for the grill.

Up to two hours ahead:
Prepare the béarnaise sauce and let stand at room temperature.

As the party unfolds:
While the roast is on one side of the barbecue, grill the shrimp on the other side for your appetizer.

Forty-five minutes before serving:
Start the potatoes on the barbecue.

Half an hour before:
Remove the roast and grill the tomatoes. The zucchini rolls can reheat on the top rack.

Between courses:
Turn the heat to MEDIUM/HIGH on the barbecue to burn off any residue and clean with a wire brush.
Return heat to LOW to grill the fruit and cake for dessert.

Warm Shrimp Cocktail

2 lbs	jumbo shrimp, peeled and deveined, tails intact		2 tbsp	onion, minced
2 tbsp	olive oil		1 tsp	puréed chipotle chili peppers in adobo sauce
	kosher salt and freshly ground black pepper, to taste		3 tbsp	prepared horseradish
			1 tbsp	lemon juice
For the Cocktail Sauce:			1 tsp	lemon zest
½ cup	ketchup			kosher salt, to taste
½ cup	chili sauce			

Preheat barbecue on MEDIUM. Brush or spray the cooking grids with vegetable oil to prevent sticking.

Meanwhile, combine the ingredients for the cocktail sauce in a medium bowl, and reserve. Toss the shrimp with olive oil, salt and pepper, then place on the barbecue.

Grill approximately 2-3 minutes per side, turning with tongs, until opaque and firm. Do not overcook. Serve warm with cocktail sauce.

Prime Rib of Beef with Béarnaise Sauce

8 lb	prime rib of beef, rolled and tied		1 tbsp	olive oil
2 cloves	garlic, minced		2 tbsp	fresh thyme, chopped
6 tbsp	Dijon mustard		1 tbsp	freshly ground black pepper

In a small bowl, combine the garlic, mustard, olive oil, thyme and pepper.

Pat the beef dry with paper towels, then spread the prepared mustard mixture over the surface. Let stand at room temperature for ½ hour. Meanwhile, prepare the barbecue by placing a drip pan under the cooking grids. Fill halfway with hot water, then preheat the barbecue on MEDIUM. Adjust the heat to MEDIUM/LOW, and place the prime rib on the cooking grids. Close the lid, and cook about 15 minutes per pound for medium rare. Using a meat thermometer to check doneness is a must. An initial check after an hour or so will give you a chance to assess the timing of the other dishes.

Closely monitor the level of water in the drip pan, ensuring it never runs dry. Very carefully add hot liquid to the drip pan as necessary, taking care to protect your hands with oven mitts to prevent steam burns.

When the meat is almost at the desired doneness, remove the roast from the barbecue and place it on a carving board tented with foil. Let it rest 20 minutes before carving. *Refer to the Indirect Grilling Guide, page 24*.

BÉARNAISE SAUCE:

2 tbsp	tarragon vinegar		¼ tsp	freshly cracked black pepper
2 tbsp	white vinegar		3	egg yolks, at room temperature
1 tbsp	water		¾ cup	butter, cubed, at room temperature
2	small shallots, minced			pinch salt
1 tsp	dried tarragon			dash cayenne pepper

In a small saucepan, combine vinegars, water, shallots, tarragon and cracked black pepper, and bring to a boil over MEDIUM/HIGH heat until reduced to one tablespoon. Reduce temperature to LOW and whisk the egg yolks into the reduction. Whisk in the butter one cube at a time, waiting until the butter is incorporated before each addition. Continue whisking until thickened. Season with salt and cayenne.

Zucchini Rolls

3	medium zucchinis, sliced ¼ inch thick, lengthwise		2 tbsp	sun-dried tomatoes, oil-packed, minced
1 tbsp	olive oil		1 tsp	oil, from the sun-dried tomatoes
4 oz	chèvre (soft goat cheese), at room temperature		1 tsp	fresh thyme, minced
	pinch freshly ground black pepper		2 tbsp	Parmesan cheese, freshly grated
	pinch kosher salt			

Preheat barbecue on MEDIUM. Brush both sides of sliced zucchini with olive oil and sprinkle with salt. Place the zucchini on the barbecue and grill for 4 minutes per side. *Refer to Grilling Guide, page 15* for instructions on creating the Perfect Grill Marks. When cooked, set on a wire rack to cool.

In a small bowl, combine the chèvre, salt, pepper, sun-dried tomatoes, oil and thyme.

Using a small spatula, spread the cheese mixture thinly over one side of the zucchini. Lightly roll the zucchini, and place seam side down on a small parchment lined baking sheet. Sprinkle with Parmesan cheese. Place baking sheet on top rack of barbecue for 15 minutes.

Remove to a platter and serve.

Grilled Tomatoes

4	tomatoes, halved		salt and pepper
1 clove	garlic, peeled and halved		handful fresh basil, shredded
2 tbsp	olive oil		

Break stems off tomatoes, if necessary, but do not remove core. Gently remove seeds with fingers, and set tomatoes on paper towels, cut side down for 10 minutes to drain. Rub cut side with garlic, then drizzle with olive oil and sprinkle with salt and pepper.

Place on preheated barbecue set at MEDIUM for 5 minutes. Rotate 1/4 turn and cook for another 5 minutes. Turn over, and cook another 5-10 minutes or until beginning to become tender. Remove to a platter, and sprinkle with shredded fresh basil.

Grilled Baby Potatoes

3 lbs	baby or fingerling potatoes

Grill on MEDIUM for 25-30 minutes as outlined in the *Vegetable Grilling Guide, page 20*.

Grilled Pound Cake with Grilled Fruit and Chocolate Sauce

1	sliced pound cake, store-bought or see recipe below		2 tbsp	maple syrup
4	bananas, halved lengthwise		1 tbsp	Grand Marnier
2	pears, cut in wedges		1 cup	whipping cream, whipped
8 slices	pineapple		1 cup	chocolate sauce (recipe follows)
2 tbsp	butter		24	raspberries

Preheat barbecue on MEDIUM. Clean grids thoroughly with grill brush. Generously brush or spray grids with vegetable oil. Reduce heat to LOW. In a small saucepan combine butter, maple syrup and Grand Marnier and heat gently on side burner of barbecue until butter is melted.

Place prepared fruit on the barbecue and baste with the maple syrup sauce. Turn fruit and continue to baste until tender and glazed, about 4 minutes. Remove to a platter and cut the fruit pieces in half once again.

Meanwhile, place pound cake slices on grill. Turn three times, about every minute, until nicely browned with Perfect Grill Marks *(refer to page 15)*. To assemble, place one slice of pound cake on each plate, lay 2 pieces each of banana, pear and pineapple on the cake. Drizzle with chocolate sauce, add a spoonful of whipped cream and top with 3 raspberries.

CHOCOLATE SAUCE:

1 cup	whipping cream		6 oz	bittersweet chocolate, chopped

In a small saucepan, bring cream to a simmer over MEDIUM heat. Remove from heat, add chocolate and whisk until smooth.

PEGGY'S POUND CAKE:

This delicious cake can be made in a 10" tube pan or 2 loaf pans.

1 cup	unsalted butter, softened		¼ tsp	baking soda
2⅔ cups	sugar		1 cup	sour cream
6	large eggs		1 tsp	vanilla
3 cups	cake flour, sifted			grated zest of 1 orange
½ tsp	salt		2 tbsp	orange juice

Grease a 10" tube pan or 2 loaf pans and dust with flour. Preheat oven to 350°F.

In a large bowl (preferably using a standing mixer) cream together the butter and sugar until very light, at least 5 minutes on medium speed. Add eggs one at a time, beating thoroughly after each and continue beating until very light.

Sift dry ingredients. Combine sour cream, vanilla, orange zest and juice in a small bowl. Alternately add sour cream and dry ingredients to the egg mixture, folding gently. Pour into prepared pan(s).

Bake for 1 hour. Place on wire rack to cool 20 minutes. Gently release from pans.

at last...

LEMONADE

•

GRILLED CHICKEN WINGS WITH
ROQUEFORT DIP AND VEGGIES

•

PEPPERONI THREE CHEESE PIZZA

•

GRILLED CINNAMON CHIPS WITH
FRUIT SALSA

•

POPSICLES

SERVES 8

The last day of school marks the first day of summer fun. The kids will not be the only ones jumping for joy when you see how easy this menu is. Kick off the party with appetizing finger food that everyone will devour. And remember that essential harbinger of long, hot, lazy days – Lemonade!

GETTING ORGANIZED

Up to one day ahead:
Marinate chicken wings, prepare Roquefort dip, grate cheese for pizza. If you are making the pizza dough from scratch, you could do it now and store it in the refrigerator overnight. Make Lemonade.

Up to two hours ahead:
Cut up celery and carrots, prepare fruit salsa and grilled cinnamon chips.

Immediately before serving:
Place pizza stone on one side of cold barbecue, then preheat barbecue on MEDIUM/HIGH.
Reduce temperature and grill chicken wings and pizza as directed in recipes.

Lemonade

1 cup	water		4 cups	cold water
1 cup	sugar			mint leaves for garnish
6	lemons			

Squeeze the juice of 5 lemons or enough to generate 1 cup of fresh juice.

Prepare a simple sugar syrup by gently heating 1 cup water and 1 cup sugar plus the rinds of 2 lemons cut into chunks in a medium saucepan. Continue cooking until sugar dissolves. Let cool, strain, then stir in lemon juice and 4 cups cold water. Just before serving, pour into a large glass pitcher over lots of ice, and garnish with lemon slices and mint leaves.

Grilled Chicken Wings with Roquefort Dip and Veggies

3 lbs	chicken wings		1 tsp	chili powder
For the Marinade:			1 tsp	oregano
⅓ cup	vegetable oil		1 tsp	kosher salt
1 clove	garlic, minced		2 tbsp	red wine vinegar
¼ tsp	cayenne			

Preheat the barbecue on HIGH. Cut each wing at the joint to make two pieces.

In a large bowl, whisk together vegetable oil, garlic, spices and vinegar. Add chicken wings and toss to coat.

Lightly brush cooking grids on one side of the barbecue with oil, reduce heat to MEDIUM and cook wings, turning to set grill marks, about 15 minutes. Move the wings up to the upper rack and continue cooking 15-20 minutes until cooked through and tender.

ROQUEFORT DIP AND VEGGIES:

½ cup	mayonnaise		1 tbsp	red wine vinegar
1 clove	garlic, minced		⅓ cup	Roquefort cheese, crumbled
1 tbsp	onion, grated			celery and carrot sticks
1 tsp	fresh thyme, chopped			

Stir together all of the dip ingredients. May be made ahead of time and chilled until ready to serve with chicken wings, celery and carrots.

Pizza Dough

1¼ tsp	active dry yeast		1 tbsp	olive oil
1 cup	lukewarm water		½ tsp	salt
2 cups	unbleached flour		½ tsp	sugar

Dissolve the yeast in lukewarm water with ½ teaspoon sugar. Add the flour, olive oil and salt and knead until elastic.
Let rest 10 minutes before rolling. No rising is required.

Pepperoni and 3 Cheese Pizza

This recipe makes two pizzas.

	pizza dough (double recipe)	½ cup	Asiago cheese, grated
	can substitute 2 balls store bought frozen dough, thawed	½ cup	Parmesan cheese, grated
1 cup	pizza sauce	½ lb	pepperoni slices
1 cup	mozzarella cheese, grated		

Preheat pizza stone by placing in cold barbecue and setting barbecue to MEDIUM/HIGH, allowing it to heat up for 10 minutes.

Prepare pizza dough by gently kneading and stretching thawed dough into desired shape, on a wooden pizza board or rimless baking tray, which has been liberally dusted with corn meal. Spread pizza sauce evenly over surface of dough and arrange pepperoni slices over sauce. Sprinkle grated cheeses evenly on top. Slide the pizza onto the hot pizza stone, using a quick movement. Reduce heat to MEDIUM and close the grill lid. Cook for 12-15 minutes, or until dough is crispy.

Grilled Cinnamon Chips with Fruit Salsa

6	flour tortillas	¼ cup	cinnamon
½ cup	sugar	¼ cup	vegetable oil, or melted butter

Preheat barbecue on MEDIUM. Brush tortillas with vegetable oil on both sides. Combine sugar and cinnamon into a small bowl. Sprinkle one side with sugar/cinnamon mixture and grill 2 minutes. Turn and sprinkle with more sugar/cinnamon mixture and grill 2 minutes more. Remove from grill, cut into bite size wedges and serve with fruit salsa.

FRUIT SALSA:

3	peaches, peeled and diced	1 tsp	honey
1 cup	raspberries	¼ tsp	cinnamon
1½ tbsp	lime juice		

Clean and prepare fruit and toss into a large bowl with honey, lime juice and cinnamon. Serve garnished with lime slices and mint if desired.

manning the grill...

Leafy Greens with
Avocado and Cherry Tomatoes

•

Orange Ginger Baby Back Ribs

•

Grilled French Fries

•

Green Beans with Toasted Almonds

•

Grilled Pineapple Upside-Down Cake

SERVES 8

It's all about Dad's favourites on Father's Day. While everyone relaxes and enjoys the serenity of your backyard, the ribs will be slowly cooking to mouth-watering perfection. This delicious menu is simple to prepare.

GETTING ORGANIZED

Up to one day ahead:
Toast almonds, prepare BBQ Sauce and vinaigrette.

The morning of:
Bake/grill cake, clean and cut potatoes for French fries and soak in a large bowl of cold, salted water.

2½ hours ahead:
Begin to grill ribs.

Immediately before serving:
Grill potatoes, prepare beans, assemble salad.

Leafy Greens with Avocado and Cherry Tomatoes

8 cups	salad greens		½ tsp	ground cumin
2	avocados		1 tsp	honey
1 cup	cherry tomatoes			pinch kosher salt
½	red onion, sliced thinly			a few grinds of black pepper
Cilantro and avocado oil vinaigrette:			1 tbsp	cider vinegar
2 tbsp	cilantro, finely chopped		1 tbsp	fresh lime juice
			¼ cup	avocado oil, or olive oil

Prepare vinaigrette by combining ingredients in a large glass bottle. Shake vigorously. Toss greens in a large bowl with sliced avocados, cherry tomatoes and red onion slices. Drizzle with vinaigrette when ready to serve.

Orange-Ginger Baby Back Ribs

5 lbs	baby back ribs		2 tbsp	orange juice
For the sauce:			2 tbsp	asian chili sauce
1 cup	ketchup		1 tbsp	Worcestershire sauce
½ cup	hoisin sauce		4 cloves	garlic, minced
4 tbsp	soy sauce		1 tbsp	ginger
2 tbsp	grainy mustard			grated zest of an orange
3 tbsp	honey			salt and pepper

Preheat barbecue on MEDIUM and turn down to LOW. Prepare ribs for grilling by removing the membrane from the underside of the ribs. Prepare several foil envelopes and place 2 strips of ribs into each envelope, with 1/4 cup of water and seal tightly. Cook for 2-21/2 hours on LOW (300°F) with the lid closed. Check the thermometer on the front of the grill lid frequently and adjust the cooking temperature accordingly. This may require turning one or two burners off and cooking indirectly.

To prepare sauce: Combine all ingredients in a saucepan and set aside until ribs are ready to remove from foil. Gently heat sauce on the sideburner for 10-15 minutes before using.

Carefully remove ribs from foil and place on grids. Baste generously with sauce, and grill for 10 minutes per side, leaving the lid open, turning several times, and basting with sauce after each turn.

Remaining sauce should be heated to a boil and then allowed to simmer for 5 -10 minutes and served on the side as a dipping sauce.

Grilled French Fries

3 lbs	potatoes, Yukon Gold
4 tbsp	olive oil
	salt and pepper

Preheat barbecue on MEDIUM for 5 minutes. Scrub potatoes and pat dry. Slice into wedges, keeping skin intact. If preparing ahead, soak in a large bowl of cold water. Drain well and pat dry.

Toss in a large glass bowl with olive oil, salt and pepper. Spread evenly over an oiled Grill Topper, or baking sheet, and place directly on top of grids. Grill for 30 minutes, turning once.

Green Beans with Toasted Almonds

1½–2 lbs	green beans, trimmed	1 tbsp	butter
¼ cup	slivered almonds, toasted	½ tsp	kosher salt

Steam or boil green beans 5-6 minutes until tender-crisp. Drain well. Return to pan and toss with almonds, butter and salt.

Grilled Pineapple Upside-Down Cake

¼ cup	butter	**For the batter:**	
½ cup	brown sugar	⅓ cup	butter
½ tsp	cinnamon	½ cup	sugar
½ tsp	fresh ginger, grated	2	eggs, beaten lightly
1 tsp	lemon juice, freshly squeezed	½ tsp	vanilla
6 slices	fresh pineapple , or substitute: 3 apples, pears or other firm fresh fruit, peeled and sliced	¼ tsp	salt
		1¼ cups	flour, all-purpose
6	maraschino cherries	2 tsp	baking powder

Preheat barbecue on MEDIUM for 10 minutes. Adjust heat setting so that oven thermometer consistently reads 350°F. This may require turning off a burner.

Mix together the butter, sugar, cinnamon and ginger, and spread on the bottom of a heavy grill-proof 10" baking pan, preferably cast iron or coated cast iron. Arrange the fruit on top and sprinkle with lemon juice.

In a separate mixing bowl, combine butter and sugar, and beat until light and fluffy. Add the eggs, vanilla and salt and stir until smooth. Add flour and baking powder and beat for one minute. Pour the batter over the fruit layer.

Place pan on the left side of the grill and turn off left burner. Close the lid and cook until the top of the cake springs back, about 45 minutes. Monitor the thermometer on the front of the grill lid frequently and adjust the cooking temperature to maintain a temperature of 350°F.

NOTE: *Can be served warm with vanilla ice cream.*

Canada day...

Iced Tea

•

Fiery Beef Burgers

•

Guacamole

•

Lemony Chicken Burgers with
Roasted Red Pepper Sauce

•

Sliced Tomatoes

•

Spicy Asian Noodle Salad

•

S'mores

Serves 8

The excitement begins early when an evening of fireworks is on the agenda.
Keep the kids occupied with games while you prepare this tasty meal.
Then it is s'mores all around when the fireworks begin on this magical evening.

GETTING ORGANIZED

Up to a day ahead:
Mix and shape the burger patties.
Prepare Roasted Red Pepper Sauce.

The morning of:
Prepare guacamole and Spicy Asian Noodle Salad.

Immediately before serving:
Grill burgers, and slice tomatoes. Toast marshmallows for S'mores.

Fiery Beef Burgers

2 lbs	lean ground beef		¾ cup	monterey jack or medium cheddar cheese, grated
¼ cup	cilantro, chopped		1 tsp	cumin
2 cloves	garlic, minced		1 tsp	kosher salt
2	jalapeno peppers, minced		8	buns

In a large bowl, lightly mix the meat with the seasoning ingredients and the cheese using your fingertips. Shape into 8 patties.

Preheat barbecue on MEDIUM/HIGH, then brush or spray grids with vegetable oil.

Place patties on the barbecue, and sear 2 minutes per side. Reduce heat to LOW and continue cooking another 2 minutes per side until juicy but cooked through. *Refer to the guide for Perfect Grill Marks, page 15*. Lightly toast the buns during the last 2 minutes of cooking time.

Guacamole

2	ripe avocados		¼ tsp	cayenne pepper
1	tomato, seeded and chopped			dash of Tabasco sauce
½	red onion, finely minced			salt and pepper
	juice of 1 lime		2 tbsp	cilantro, chopped
1 tsp	ground cumin			

Mash avocado in a medium size mixing bowl. Add chopped tomato, red onion, lime juice and Tabasco sauce. Season with blended cumin, cayenne, salt and pepper. Top with chopped cilantro.

Cover with plastic wrap, pressed directly against the guacamole, to prevent browning, and refrigerate until ready to serve.

Lemony Chicken Burgers with Roasted Red Pepper Sauce

2 lbs	ground chicken		4 tsp	lemon zest
1 lb	frozen spinach, thawed, drained and chopped		2 cloves	garlic, minced
6	green onions, chopped		1 tsp	paprika
2	eggs, lightly beaten			salt and pepper, to taste
6 tbsp	parmesan cheese		8	sesame seed buns

In a large mixing bowl, lightly mix ground chicken, spinach, green onion, egg, parmesan cheese, lemon zest, garlic, paprika, salt & pepper. Form into 8 patties and chill for 30 minutes.

To grill burgers: Preheat barbecue on MEDIUM/HIGH, and oil the grids generously to prevent sticking. Place the patties on the grill, and reduce heat to MEDIUM. Place patties on the barbecue, and sear 3 minutes per side, taking care not to press down the patties.

Reduce heat to LOW and continue cooking for another 3 minutes per side until juicy but cooked through. *Refer to guide for Perfect Grill Marks, page 15*. Lightly toast the buns during the last 2 minutes of cooking time. Serve on toasted sesame seed buns, topped with Roasted Red Pepper Sauce.

ROASTED RED PEPPER SAUCE:

2 large	roasted red peppers (see page 20) peeled and seeded		4 tsp	Dijon mustard
			2 tsp	honey
8	green onions, chopped		1 ½ tsp	fresh basil, chopped
2 cloves	garlic, minced			salt and freshly ground black pepper, to taste
4 tbsp	olive oil			

Sauté onion and garlic very gently. Add to food processor with remaining ingredients and process until well blended.

Spicy Asian Noodle Salad

This salad is a real crowd pleaser. You can buy chili oil in the supermarket if you like, but if you make a batch of ours, you will have lots left to make more salad dressing! It is also excellent for rubbing on meat before grilling, and can be stored for up to two months.

Salad:

1 pkg	(300 g) dried steamed egg noodles
1 cup	broccoli florets
½	red pepper, julienned
½	small red onion, thinly sliced
2	carrots, peeled and julienned
2 tbsp	cilantro, chopped
2 tbsp	toasted sesame seeds
	salt and pepper, to taste

Asian Noodle Dressing:

½ cup	soy sauce
3 tbsp	rice vinegar
3 tbsp	sesame oil
½ cup	chili oil (see recipe below)

Cook noodles and broccoli florets in a large pot of salted, rapidly boiling water for 3½ minutes.
Drain and cool down quickly under cold running water. Place in a large bowl and add red peppers, red onions and carrots.
Combine all of the dressing ingredients in a glass jar with a tight fitting lid and shake vigorously. Toss salad with ½ cup of dressing, adding more as desired.
Season with salt and pepper, garnish with toasted sesame seeds and chopped cilantro.

CHILI OIL:

1 ½ cups	canola oil
3	whole thai chili peppers
2 tsp	ginger (unpeeled), chopped
2 cloves	garlic, peeled
½ tsp	coriander seed
½ tsp	fennel seeds
½ tsp	black peppercorns

Put all ingredients in a pot and simmer for 2 hours. Do not let boil. Turn off heat and let cool. Strain and store in a glass jar, in a cool, dark cupboard.

S'Mores

graham crackers
large marshmallows
large semi-sweet or milk chocolate bar, broken into squares

Preheat grill on MEDIUM for 10 minutes. Place marshmallow on end of long stick, hold over grids and toast until it is golden brown on the outside, and soft and gooey on the inside. Create a "sandwich" by placing the hot marshmallow between a graham cracker and a piece of chocolate.
The heat of the marshmallow will soften the chocolate, creating a sweet, molten treat!

Iced Tea

4	earl grey tea bags
8 cups	boiling water
½ cup	honey, or sugar
2	lemons, thinly sliced

Steep tea in boiling water for 5 minutes. Remove tea bags and stir in honey, or sugar. Chill. To serve, add ice to drinking glasses, fill with tea and garnish with 2 lemon slices per glass.

sweet legacy...

MIMOSAS

•

GRILLED SCALLOPS WITH MANGO SAUCE

•

BABY GREENS WITH ROASTED RED PEPPER,
CHÈVRE AND HONEY PECANS

•

CEDAR PLANK SALMON
WITH ASIAN GINGER MARINADE

•

MARINATED ASPARAGUS SALAD
WITH TOASTED SESAME SEEDS

•

GRILLED BABY POTATOES

•

GRILLED CORN BREAD SQUARES

•

COUSIN MELISSA'S BLUEBERRY CAKE

SERVES 8

This simple, yet elegant seafood menu will delight your lunch or dinner guests. Tender scallops with a tangy mango sauce are a unique way to start the party. Serve them as an appetizer or as part of your buffet.
Cedar plank salmon is a great choice for serving a crowd as it is simple to prepare and needs so little tending.
The blueberry cake recipe takes advantage of seasonal summer freshness, and can, along with the cornbread, serve up to 16 people.
Each recipe stands alone as a classic that can be savoured at any gathering
and can easily be scaled up, even quadrupled, for a larger crowd.

GETTING ORGANIZED

Up to one week ahead:
Make and freeze the corn bread and honey pecans.

Up to one day ahead:
Make mango sauce, marinade for the salmon and dressings for the salads.
You can also make the blueberry cake, blanch the asparagus, and roast the red peppers for the salad.

As the party unfolds:
Pour the Mimosas and man the barbecue for the scallops, then salmon, potatoes, and corn bread!

Immediately before serving:
Toss the salad and arrange the asparagus.

Mimosas

| 1 | bottle chilled Champagne |
| | chilled fresh orange juice |

Into each champagne flute, pour 3 ounces champagne and top with 2 ounces fresh orange juice. Swirl to mix.

Grilled Scallops with Mango Sauce

2 lbs	large scallops	2	cloves garlic, roughly chopped
2 tsp	vegetable oil	2 tbsp	rice vinegar
	salt and freshly ground pepper	2 tbsp	canola oil
For the Sauce:		½ tsp	asian chili sauce
1	large, ripe mango, peeled and cubed		cilantro or mint leaves, for garnish
1 tbsp	ginger root, peeled and grated		

Rinse scallops, pat dry with paper towels and remove the side "muscle" if attached. Toss the scallops with 2 teaspoons vegetable oil and salt and pepper in a medium bowl. Set aside.

In a blender or food processor, puree the mango, ginger root, garlic and rice vinegar. Add canola oil and chili sauce and blend together. Add salt and pepper as well as rice vinegar to taste.

On a preheated barbecue set at MEDIUM, grill the scallops quickly, about 1½ - 2 minutes per side. Drizzle a little Mango Sauce into individual martini glasses, then add 2 scallops and drizzle with more Mango Sauce. Garnish with a sprig of fresh cilantro or mint.

Baby Greens with Roasted Red Pepper, Chèvre and Honey Pecans

5 cups	baby greens	*For the Herb and Walnut Oil Vinaigrette*:	
2 cups	arugula	1	small shallot
1	roasted red pepper, thinly sliced (see vegetable grilling guide, p 20)	2	cloves garlic
		2 tbsp	fresh ginger, finely minced
1½ oz	chèvre cheese, crumbled	2 tbsp	cilantro, chopped
For the Honey Pecans:		¼ cup	walnut oil
2 cups	pecans	4 tbsp	red wine vinegar
¼ cup	honey	2 tbsp	soy sauce
¼ cus	sugar		salt and pepper, to taste
¼ tsp	salt		
¼ cup	water		

For Honey Pecans: Preheat oven to 350°F. Line baking sheet with parchment paper and spray with vegetable oil cooking spray. Combine honey, sugar, salt and water in a medium saucepan, add pecans, and cook until honey/sugar mixture is dry and totally covering the nuts. Spread pecans on baking sheet, bake for 15 minutes, turning every 5 minutes.

Prepare vinaigrette: Mince shallot, garlic and ginger in a small blender. Add walnut oil, red wine vinegar, soy sauce, cilantro, salt and pepper. Blend thoroughly.

Assemble salad: Combine greens and arugula in a large bowl and toss with vinaigrette. Top with red pepper, crumbled chèvre and honey pecans.

Cedar Plank Grilled Salmon with Asian Ginger Marinade

1 6lb	salmon fillet, skin-on		1 tsp	honey
Asian Ginger Marinade:			1 tsp	asian chili sauce
¼ cup	white wine			salt and pepper, to taste
1	orange, finely grated zest and juice		1	untreated cedar plank,
1 tbsp	sesame oil			sized to accommodate salmon fillet
1 tsp	ginger, grated			

To begin with, soak an untreated piece of cedar in a container of water for at least an hour. You may need to place a weight on top to keep the wood immersed.

Meanwhile, combine ingredients for marinade in a large, flat shallow glass dish and marinate the salmon fillets, skin-on, in the refrigerator for half an hour. Preheat barbecue on HIGH for 10 minutes.

Pat dry plank and oil the upper side. Place plank directly on the grids and heat with the lid closed until the plank begins to smoke. Place the salmon, skin side down in the middle of the plank and grill until just opaque at the thickest part. A 6 lb. fillet may take 30 minutes.

Marinated Asparagus with Toasted Sesame Seeds

2 lbs	asparagus, washed and trimmed			juice of ½ lemon
For the dressing:			1 tbsp	balsamic vinegar
1	small shallot			freshly ground black pepper, to taste
1	small clove garlic		½ cup	mild olive oil
½ tsp	salt		2 tbsp	sesame seeds, toasted
1½ tsp	Dijon mustard			

To blanch the asparagus, bring a large pot of salted water to a boil on High. Place one pound of asparagus in the boiling water for 2 minutes, remove with tongs and plunge into ice water for 2 minutes, then drain on paper towel lined wire racks, blotting off any moisture with more paper towels. Let stand at room temperature and repeat with the second pound of asparagus.

For the dressing: Pulse the shallot and the garlic in the bowl of a food processor until finely chopped. Add the salt, mustard, lemon juice, vinegar, and pepper, and process briefly to combine. With the motor running, add the olive oil in a thin stream.

Half an hour before serving, arrange the asparagus on a platter and drizzle with the vinaigrette dressing. Sprinkle with toasted sesame seeds. Serve at room temperature.

Grilled Baby Potatoes

3 lbs	baby potatoes
2 tbsp	olive oil
	salt

Preheat barbecue on MEDIUM. Wash potatoes and toss with olive oil and salt. Place on grids, and cook with lid closed for 30 minutes, turning occasionally.

Grilled Cornbread Squares

1½ cups	cornmeal		1 tsp	salt
1 cup	unbleached flour		1½ cups	buttermilk
⅓ cup	sugar		2	eggs, lightly beaten
1 tbsp	baking powder		¾ cup	butter, melted and cooled

Preheat oven to 400°F. Grease a 9" square baking pan.

Combine cornmeal, flour, sugar, baking powder and salt in a large bowl. Mix buttermilk, eggs and melted butter in a medium bowl. Stir the wet ingredients into the dry ingredients, taking care not to over mix. Spoon the batter into the prepared pan. Bake until golden, about 25 minutes.

Let cool on wire rack for 10 minutes, then turn out and cool completely. At this point the cornbread can be wrapped well and frozen or refrigerated until ready to serve.

To grill the cornbread: Cut into large squares and place on preheated, oiled barbecue turning to grill on all sides and heat through.

Cousin Melissa's Blueberry Cake

¼ lb	butter, softened		½ tsp	salt
¾ cup	sugar		2 cups	blueberries
1	egg		For the Topping:	
½ cup	milk		¼ cup	white sugar
1 tsp	vanilla		¼ cup	brown sugar
2 cups	unbleached flour		2 tbsp	butter
2 tsp	baking powder		½ tsp	cinnamon

Preheat oven to 350°F and butter the bottom and sides of a 9" x 9" cake pan.

Cream butter and sugar with an electric mixer until light and fluffy. Beat in egg. Stir in milk and vanilla until blended.

In a small bowl combine flour, salt and baking powder, and with a few swift strokes mix this into the butter and egg mixture. Gently fold in blueberries. Spoon into the prepared pan.

In a small bowl, lightly mix the topping ingredients with a fork until crumbly. Sprinkle over the cake batter.

Bake 50 minutes. Cool on rack and cut into squares to serve.

making a splash...

Fresh Vegetable Crudités
with Red Curry, Coconut
and Peanut Dip

•

Indonesian Pork Brochettes
with Naan Bread

•

Korean Chicken Wraps

•

Chocolate Chip Cookies

Serves 8

A picnic can spirit you away to a calmer place! Pack up this portable spread and head for your favourite oasis or, even closer to home, your backyard sanctuary. You'll make a splash with these delicate asian flavours. Watch as adults and kids enjoy these healthy, flavourful finger foods in the fresh outdoor air.

GETTING ORGANIZED

Up to a day ahead:
Prepare dips, marinate and grill chicken and pork, and bake cookies.

Immediately before packing the picnic:
Cut up vegetables, and assemble wraps.

Fresh Vegetable Crudités with Red Curry, Coconut and Peanut Dip

This spicy dip is also excellent with chicken or beef satays, so save any leftovers for the next day's meal! To make satays, thread thin strips of beef or chicken on skewers and grill according to *Direct Grilling Guide, page 17.*

2	red peppers	1½ tbsp	rice vinegar
3	carrots	1 tsp	brown sugar
3	celery stalks	1 can	coconut milk
2 cups	broccoli florets	1 tbsp	soy sauce
1 cup	grape tomatoes	3 tbsp	peanut butter*
For the dip:			juice of ½ lime
1 tsp	olive oil		salt and pepper
4 cloves	garlic, finely minced		
2 tsp	red curry paste		

Cut vegetables into kid friendly crudités.

For the dip: Cook garlic and red curry paste in 1 teaspoon olive oil. Add rice vinegar, brown sugar, coconut milk and soy sauce. Bring to a simmer over low heat.

Add peanut butter and whisk gently. Reduce over low heat until thick. Watch carefully, as this sauce burns easily.

Add lime juice and salt and pepper

If there are any concerns about peanut allergies, substitute with soy butter.

Indonesian Pork Brochettes with Naan Bread

1½ lbs	pork loin, boneless, sliced into ½-inch thick strips	2 cloves	fresh garlic, minced
For marinade:		2 tsp	fresh ginger, minced
1 can	coconut milk	2 tsp	soy sauce
6	green onions, chopped	1	fresh lime, juice and zest
2 stalks	lemongrass (substitute lemongrass in a jar, packed in water), peeled and chopped	1 tsp	honey
2	red chili peppers (substitute 1 tsp asian chili paste), seeded and minced	24	bamboo skewers
		8 pieces	Naan bread

In a large glass bowl, combine marinade ingredients, and add prepared pork strips.

Allow to marinate, covered, in the refrigerator for at least 2 hours. Meanwhile, soak bamboo skewers in water, so they will not char while grilling. Preheat the barbecue on MEDIUM, and brush grids with oil to prevent sticking.

Thread pork strips onto skewers, reserving marinade. Place the brochettes on the hot grids and grill approximately 4 minutes per side, turning once.

Place reserved marinade in a small sauce pan and heat to boiling. Reduce heat and cook for 5 minutes until sauce thickens slightly.

Serve brochettes and Naan bread with marinade in a dipping bowl. Garnish with lime slices and chopped green onions.

NOTE: *It is always important to boil marinade to destroy any bacteria transferred from the raw meat!*

Korean Chicken Wraps

8	chicken breasts, skinless, boneless		*Filling*:	
Korean Barbecue Sauce:			4 oz	rice vermicelli
½ cup	hoisin sauce, bottled		2 heads	green leaf lettuce, separated into leaves, substitute Boston lettuce
¼ cup	soy sauce, low-sodium		1	cucumber, cut into 2 inch matchsticks
2 tbsps	honey		2 cups	bean sprouts
1 tbsp	rice vinegar		3	green onions, chopped
1 tbsp	fresh ginger, minced			fresh cilantro, small bunch
1 tbsp	asian chili sauce		1	lime, cut into wedges
1 tbsp	sesame oil			
2 cloves	garlic, minced			

For the Korean Barbecue Sauce: Combine the hoisin sauce, soy sauce, honey, rice vinegar, ginger, asian chili sauce, sesame oil and garlic in a glass bowl. This can be made ahead, covered and refrigerated for 1 week.

Prepare chicken by marinating with ½ of Korean Barbecue Sauce in a glass dish, covered, for 3 hours or overnight.

Meanwhile, prepare rice vermicelli by cooking in a large pot of boiling water until tender, for approximately 1 minute. Drain and toss with a couple of teaspoons of Korean Barbecue Sauce.

Preheat the barbecue on MEDIUM. Brush grids with vegetable oil. Place chicken breasts on the grill and cook for 12 minutes, turning once halfway through cooking. Transfer the chicken to a cutting board , let rest for 5 minutes, then slice into strips.

To assemble Wraps: Lay lettuce leaves on a flat surface and layer with chicken strips, rice vermicelli, bean sprouts, cucumber and green onion. Top with Korean Barbecue Sauce. Garnish with fresh cilantro leaves and lime wedges. Roll up, wrap in a square of wax paper and go! Enjoy your picnic!

Chocolate Chip Cookies

½ cup	shortening		1¾ cups	unbleached flour
¼ cup	butter, at room temperature		1 tsp	salt
1¼ cups	brown sugar, lightly packed		1 tsp	baking soda
1	egg		1 cup	chocolate chips
1 tbsp	milk		1 cup	pecans, coarsely chopped
2 tsp	vanilla			

Preheat oven to 375°F.

In a large bowl, cream together shortening, butter, and sugar, and beat until light, about 2 minutes.

Add egg, milk, and vanilla, and beat for another minute.

Combine flour, salt and baking soda and add to the creamed mixture. Mix until just blended. Stir in chocolate chips and pecans.

Drop big heaping spoonfuls onto an ungreased baking sheet, spacing well apart. Bake 10 minutes until golden in colour, but still appearing moist. Cool 2 minutes on sheet, then transfer to a wire rack to cool completely.

sugar & spice...

Cosmopolitans

•

Seared Tuna Burgers with
Wasabi Flavoured Mayonnaise

•

Asian Coleslaw

•

Watermelon Daiquiri Balls

Serves 8

Getting the girls together for an evening in is a rare and special occasion.
This light, simple fare lets you focus on the fun and laughter.
This menu is full of fresh, crisp and light flavours and a refreshing girlie drink to round off the meal!

GETTING ORGANIZED

Up to six hours ahead:
Prepare the Watermelon Daiquiri Balls, refrigerate and let the flavours infuse throughout the day.
Prepare the Wasabi Mayonnaise and the dressing for the coleslaw.

Immediately before serving:
The burgers and coleslaw can be whipped up quickly.
Why not start the cosmos going in the kitchen while you all pitch in?

Cosmopolitans

This recipe is for 2 cocktails.

Vodka

Triple Sec

cranberry juice

fresh lime juice

limes

ice

Run a cut slice of lime around the rim of a martini glass. Dip rim into a plate of sugar to coat. In a cocktail shaker filled with ice, add 3 oz Vodka, 2 oz Triple Sec, 5 oz cranberry juice cocktail and 1 oz lime juice. Shake and strain into prepared martini glasses. Garnish with a lime slice.

Seared Tuna Burgers with Wasabi Flavoured Mayonnaise

8 - ¾"	thick tuna steaks
3 tbsp	sesame oil
1½ tbsp	kosher salt
1½ tbsp	freshly ground black pepper
3 tbsp	sesame seeds

For the Mayonnaise:

⅔ cup	mayonnaise

2 tbsp	prepared wasabi (available in tubes in specialty grocery stores)
2 cloves	garlic, minced
2 tbsp	cilantro, chopped
1	small bunch arugula
8	plain buns

Preheat barbecue on MEDIUM. Pat dry tuna steaks. Brush with sesame oil, and sprinkle with salt, pepper and sesame seeds.

Meanwhile, prepare the mayonnaise by combining the mayonnaise, wasabi, garlic and cilantro in a small bowl.

Brush or spray cooking grids with vegetable oil. Place tuna on the grill for 1½ - 2 minutes per side, (refer to the Direct Grilling Guide, page 18) until seared outside and rare inside. At the same time, toast the buns on the upper rack. Spread the buns with mayonnaise, place tuna on the bun and top with arugula.

Asian Coleslaw

2 cups	shredded green cabbage
2 cups	shredded purple cabbage
1 cup	shredded carrots
1	red pepper, julienned
1	cucumber, julienned
4	green onions, finely chopped
2 tbsp	fresh cilantro, finely chopped

Dressing:

3 tbsp	vegetable oil
3 tbsp	soy sauce
1 tbsp	sesame oil

2 tbsp	rice wine vinegar
1 tsp	lime juice
1 tsp	garlic, minced
1 tsp	brown sugar
1 tsp	chili powder
1	green onion, finely chopped
¼ tsp	red pepper flakes
	salt and pepper, to taste
2 tbsp	toasted sesame seeds

In a large bowl, combine cabbage, carrots, cucumber, green onions and coriander. In a small bowl, combine vegetable oil, soy sauce, sesame oil, rice wine vinegar, lime juice, garlic, brown sugar, chili powder, green onion and red pepper flakes. Whisk until blended.

Just before serving, pour dressing over slaw and toss. Sprinkle with toasted sesame seeds.

Watermelon Daiquiri Balls

1	Seedless watermelon	4	limes, freshly squeezed
8 oz	white rum		mint, for garnish
8 tsp	sugar		

Slice top ⅓ off watermelon, lengthwise. Using melon baller, carefully scoop out flesh of watermelon and place in a large glass bowl, creating as many melon balls as possible, from both parts of the watermelon. Discard top rind. Scrape out remaining bits of flesh from the large piece of watermelon. This will act as the serving vessel for the watermelon balls. Cover with plastic wrap and refrigerate until ready to assemble.

Combine white rum, sugar and lime juice in a glass container and shake. Pour carefully over watermelon balls, allowing rum solution to infuse into the watermelon. Chill watermelon balls for 2-3 hours. Before serving, place watermelon balls into watermelon basket and garnish with a large sprig of mint.

NOTE: Any remaining juice can be served on ice, as watermelon daiquiris!

a promising
affair...

82

Pancetta Wrapped Shrimp

•

Caramelized Onion Mini Pizzas with
Gorgonzola Cheese and Hot Capicolla

•

Beef Tenderloin

•

Chipotle Sauce

•

Roasted Rosemary Potatoes

•

Green Bean Salad

•

Grilled Vegetable Stacks

•

Caesar Salad

•

Flourless Chocolate Cake with
Chocolate Glaze

Serves 8

When celebrating an important milestone, pull together a special menu that you know will work. This classic menu of timeless favourites can easily be scaled up to accommodate a large number of guests. The many make-ahead items will allow you to easily pace the rest of the preparations on the special day. Since many of the dishes are as tasty cold as they are hot, timing is less critical. For this feast the barbecue will hold centre stage, so appoint a willing chef to pitch in to help with the grilling.

GETTING ORGANIZED

Up to one week ahead:
Bake and freeze the chocolate cake. Prepare pizza dough and form into 2" mini pizzas. Brush both sides with olive oil, and place them directly on a hot grill, turning once. Let cool, and store in a tightly sealed container in the freezer until ready to assemble and grill with the toppings.

Up to one day ahead:
Caramelize the onions, make the Chipotle Sauce, prepare the vinaigrette for the bean salad, blanch the beans, and grill the vegetables for the stacks. Mix ricotta cheese spread for the Vegetable Stacks.

The morning of the party:
Glaze the cake. Bring the vegetables back to room temperature, then assemble the stacks.
Make the Caesar Salad Dressing and cook the bacon. Thaw the pizza shells and assemble with toppings.

As the party unfolds:
Marinate, assemble and grill the shrimp, which can be served hot or at room temperature, grill the beef and roast the potatoes. During the first resting stage of the beef, reheat the pizzas and serve. During the final resting of the beef, reheat the Vegetable Stacks.

Immediately before serving:
Assemble the Green Bean Salad and the Caesar Salad.

Pancetta Wrapped Shrimp

2 tsp	paprika	½ tsp	freshly ground black pepper
½ tsp	cayenne	1 tbsp	olive oil
½ tsp	curry powder	2 tbsp	white sugar
½ tsp	ground cumin	2 tbsp	fresh lemon juice
½ tsp	ground coriander	24	jumbo shrimp, shelled and deveined
½ tsp	salt	12	thin slices lean pancetta, sliced in half

Preheat barbecue on MEDIUM for 10 minutes. Combine the first 10 ingredients in a medium sized mixing bowl. Add the shrimp and marinate for 30 minutes. Wrap the shrimp with the pancetta, securing with a toothpick if necessary.

Brush the cooking grids with olive or vegetable oil. Grill shrimp 2 - 3 minutes per side, until the shrimp becomes opaque and curls.

Caramelized Onion Mini Pizzas with Gorgonzola Cheese and Hot Capicolla

1 recipe	pizza dough (see page 46) or 1 batch frozen pizza dough, thawed	5 slices	hot capicolla ham, chopped
3	large onions, roughly chopped	¼ cup	fresh basil, chiffonade
2 tbsp	olive oil		coarse salt
1 cup	crumbled Gorgonzola cheese		

Shape and grill the mini pizzas as outlined in *Getting Organized (page 85)*. If frozen ahead, thaw the prepared mini crusts before proceeding with the recipe.

Heat olive oil in a large sauté pan and add the onions. Cook on LOW for 30 - 40 minutes, stirring occasionally, until the onions are very soft and golden brown. Top pizza crusts with onion, Gorgonzola cheese and capicolla.

Bake on a cookie sheet in a preheated 400°F oven or barbecue until the cheese is melted and pizzas are heated through. Garnish with basil chiffonade and a sprinkle of coarse salt.

Beef Tenderloin

1	whole beef tenderloin, at room temperature	coarse salt and freshly ground black pepper
1 tbsp	olive oil	

Preheat barbecue and set temperature to MEDIUM. Pat tenderloin dry with paper towels, and brush with olive oil. Season with salt and pepper.

Place the tenderloin on oiled barbecue grids at a 45 degree angle for 18 minutes, rotating the meat by ⅓ every 6 minutes, to get grill marks on all sides. Remove the tenderloin from the barbecue to a glass dish and tent with foil, letting it rest for 20 minutes.

Return the tenderloin to the grids, placing it on the opposite 45 degree angle. Rotate the meat by ⅓ every 6 minutes, basting it with juices from the glass dish.

Remove the tenderloin to a carving board and cover with foil and a kitchen towel to insulate. Let it rest a second time for 10 - 20 minutes to reabsorb the juices before carving.

NOTE: *Follow the "Perfect Grill Marks" instructions on page 15.*

Chipotle Sauce

This smokey, spicy mayo is wonderful with chicken, pork, fish or beef, or even as a dip for grilled vegetables.
Save leftovers for an outstanding sandwich spread.

1 cup	mayonnaise		1 tsp	puréed chipotle peppers
2 cloves	garlic, minced		½ tsp	ground cumin
1 tbsp	lemon juice		3 tbsp	cilantro, finely chopped

Combine all ingredients, cover well, and store in refrigerator until ready to use. May be stored for up to 3 days.

Roasted Rosemary Potatoes

6	large Russet or Yukon Gold potatoes, peeled and cut in 1" cubes		2 tbsp	fresh rosemary, chopped
2 tbsp	olive oil			kosher salt and freshly ground black pepper, to taste

Prepare potatoes and toss with the olive oil, rosemary, salt and pepper. Line a large rimmed baking sheet with parchment paper.

Place in 400°F oven or on barbecue and roast, turning several times, until crispy, browned and cooked through, about 40 minutes.

Sprinkle with more salt and pepper, to taste.

Green Bean Salad

2 lbs	green beans, stem ends removed		3 tbsp	apple cider vinegar
For the Vinaigrette:			½ cup	olive oil
3 tbsp	Dijon mustard		½ cup	fresh dill, finely chopped
3 tbsp	honey			salt and freshly ground black pepper, to taste
1	lemon, freshly squeezed			

Bring a large pot of salted water to a boil. Add beans and cook until just tender crisp, about 5 minutes. Drain and place beans in a bowl of ice water for 5 minutes. Drain again. Lay towels or paper towels over cooling racks. Dry beans well, then wrap them up in damp toweling, and refrigerate until ready to use. (Can be prepared one day in advance to this stage). Combine all the dressing ingredients if using the same day. If preparing more than one day in advance, omit the dill until the last minute. Arrange the beans decoratively on a platter. Just before serving, add the dill and drizzle with the dressing.

Grilled Vegetable Stacks

The key to nice presentation with this dish is using vegetables of approximately the same diameter. To make them really tidy and perfect, use a round cookie cutter to cut the vegetable and mozzarella slices to a uniform size and shape. Makes 8 stacks.

½ cup	olive oil		1 cup	ricotta cheese
4	whole red peppers			salt and pepper, to taste
2	medium eggplant, cut in 16 slices (⅓" thick)*		2 tsp	fresh thyme leaves, finely chopped
2	large zucchini, cut in 16 slices (¼" thick) crosswise		8 thick	slices mozzarella cheese
3	medium tomatoes, cut in 8 slices (⅓" thick)		8	long sprigs fresh rosemary
4	small red onions, cut in 16 slices (⅓" thick)			

Preparing the vegetables and filling: Preheat barbecue on MEDIUM/HIGH and place whole red peppers directly on the grill, charring the skin on all sides. Let cool, then peel off skins, remove seeds and ribs, and lay flat on a cutting board. Using a cookie cutter roughly the diameter of the remaining vegetables, cut 8 rounds of peppers and set aside. Freeze the scraps of red pepper to add to soups, pasta sauces, salads, etc.

Brush the remaining prepared vegetables with olive oil and season with salt and pepper. Reduce flame to LOW and grill the vegetables slowly, until tender, turning once. Transfer the vegetables to a tray, arranging them in a single layer to cool, and cover tightly with plastic wrap. The vegetables may be grilled one day in advance, and refrigerated after cooling. Bring them back to room temperature before proceeding with the recipe.

Assembly: Stir together the ricotta cheese, thyme, salt and pepper in a small bowl. Place one slice of eggplant on a lightly oiled baking sheet or foil pan. Spread a spoonful of the ricotta mixture over the eggplant. Stack with red pepper, zucchini, onion, mozzarella, tomato, another zucchini, and another onion. Spread another spoonful of ricotta over the onion and top with another slice of eggplant. Repeat this procedure with the remaining vegetables to make 7 more stacks.

Insert a wooden skewer through the center of each stack and return the vegetables to the barbecue on the baking sheet.

Heat for about 10 minutes on LOW or until the cheese is melted and the vegetables are warmed through. Remove the bottom leaves from each rosemary sprig, leaving one inch of leaves on the top. Pull out the skewers and insert one prepared rosemary sprig into the centre of each stack.

*****NOTE:** *Before cooking, place sliced eggplant on a layer of paper towels and sprinkle with salt. Cover with another layer of paper towels and let sit for 20 - 30 minutes. This removes the bitterness from the eggplant.*

Caesar Salad

1	large head romaine lettuce, washed and torn	2 cloves	peeled garlic
8 strips	bacon, cooked and crumbled	1 dash	Tabasco or other hot pepper sauce
For the Dressing:		2 dashes	Worcestershire sauce
	juice of ½ lemon		kosher salt and black pepper, to taste
2 tsp	Dijon mustard	5 tbsp	extra virgin olive oil
1	egg yolk	¼ cup	Parmesan cheese, shaved
3	anchovy fillets		

Chill plates and prepare lettuce and bacon. Set aside in refrigerator.

In a food processor, blend lemon juice, mustard, egg yolk, anchovies, garlic, Tabasco, Worcestershire, salt and pepper. With motor running, drizzle in olive oil in a thin stream.

Toss dressing with lettuce and bacon. Serve on chilled plates and garnish with shaved Parmesan.

Flourless Chocolate Cake with Chocolate Glaze

This cake is rich and dense. Top quality chocolate will yield superior results.

For the Cake:		*For the Glaze*:	
12 oz	bittersweet chocolate, chopped	⅓ cup	whipping cream
¾ cup	unsalted butter, cut into pieces	⅓ cup	corn syrup
6	large eggs, separated	7 oz	bittersweet chocolate, finely chopped
¾ cup	sugar		
2 tsp	vanilla		

Preheat oven to 350ºF.

Butter a 9" springform pan. Line bottom of pan with parchment paper, then butter the paper. To prevent any leaking, wrap the outside of the pan with aluminum foil.

In a medium saucepan over low heat, stir chocolate and butter until melted and smooth. Remove from heat and cool to lukewarm.

Beat egg yolks and half (6 tbsp) the sugar in a large bowl until thick and pale, about 3 minutes. Fold in cooled chocolate, and vanilla extract.

In a clean, dry bowl, with a whisk attachment, beat egg whites until soft peaks form. Gradually add remaining (6 tbsp) sugar until medium-firm peaks form. Do not overbeat. Fold whites into the chocolate mixture in 3 additions. Pour batter into prepared pan.

Bake cake on middle rack of oven until puffed and cracked, about 50 minutes. Cool cake in pan on a rack. The cake will fall. Gently press down on top to make an evenly thick cake. Cut around the sides of the pan to loosen the cake. Remove the sides. Invert onto cake plate, and peel off parchment paper.

To make the Glaze: In a medium saucepan bring whipping cream and corn syrup to a simmer. Remove from heat and add chocolate, whisking until melted and smooth. Pour glaze over cake, smoothing the top with a knife if desired. Can be made up to 2 days ahead, covered and refrigerated, or 1 week ahead and frozen without the glaze. Serve at room temperature, with whipped cream and berries, if desired.

catch of the day...

GRILLED PICKEREL WITH
FRESH PICO DE GALLO

•

BAKED POTATOES

•

CORN ON THE COB WITH
CAJUN BUTTER

•

BRYN'S MOM'S BUTTER TARTS

SERVES 8

Hot, lazy summer days are too precious to waste in the kitchen. Enhance your outdoor leisure time with a visit to a local farm stand to choose fresh corn and tomatoes for this effortless menu. The tangy fresh flavour of this Pico de Gallo is a perfect summer-time compliment to freshly caught pickerel, or any white fish that is available in your area of the world. If no local fish is available, halibut grills up beautifully.

GETTING ORGANIZED

Up to one day ahead:
Bake the Butter Tarts, or send someone to the bakery to pick up some tarts.
Prepare the Cajun Butter.

Up to one hour ahead:
Assemble Pico de Gallo, scrub potatoes and soak corn while preheating the grill. Bake the potatoes and corn.

Immediately before serving:
Grill fish.

Grilled Pickerel with Fresh Pico de Gallo

2	pickerel fillets		2	lemons, sliced
2 tbsp	vegetable oil or melted butter			salt and freshly ground black pepper, to taste
2 tbsp	lemon juice			

Preheat grill on MEDIUM for 10 minutes. Brush grids with oil.

Meanwhile, combine vegetable oil or melted butter, lemon juice and salt and pepper, and brush lightly over fish fillets. Place fillets on grids, close the lid and cook for 4 - 5 minutes per side, turning carefully with a large spatula. The rule of thumb is 10 minutes of grilling per inch thickness of fish fillet.

Using a fish basket makes turning a lot easier. We always grill up lemon slices to serve along side the fish. Remove fish and serve immediately with Pico de Gallo.

For the Pico de Gallo:

3	tomatoes, seeded and chopped		¼ cup	fresh cilantro, finely chopped
½	red onion, finely chopped		1 tsp	freshly squeezed lime juice
1	jalapeno pepper, seeded and diced		1 tbsp	extra virgin olive oil
1 clove	garlic, minced or pressed			dash of Tabasco sauce
				salt and pepper

Combine chopped tomatoes, onions, jalapeno peppers, garlic and cilantro in a glass bowl. Add lime juice, extra virgin olive oil, Tabasco sauce and salt and pepper. Stir and refrigerate until ready to serve.

Corn on the Cob with Cajun Butter

8 ears   fresh corn, do not husk, trim silk

Soak corn on the cob in a large pot of salted cold water for 20 minutes. Do not husk.

Preheat barbecue on MEDIUM for 10 minutes. Shake excess water off of corn and place directly on the grids.

With lid closed, cook for 20 minutes, turning once. Let cool for 5 minutes. Wearing oven mitts or gloves, remove husks and serve with Cajun Butter, salt and pepper.

CAJUN BUTTER:

4 cloves	garlic, minced		1 tbsp	Worcestershire sauce
2	shallots, minced		1 tsp	kosher salt
¼ cup	fresh basil, finely chopped		1 tsp	white pepper
1 tbsp	fresh thyme, finely chopped		¼ tsp	cayenne
1 cup	unsalted butter, room temperature			

Combine all ingredients in a medium bowl. Stir with a wooden spoon until thoroughly blended. Place Cajun Butter onto a large sheet of waxed paper and shape into a log. Refrigerate and cut into patties when chilled.

Baked Potatoes

8 medium size russet potatoes

Preheat barbecue on MEDIUM for 10 minutes. Meanwhile, scrub potatoes thoroughly to clean. Puncture several times with a fork and wrap individually in aluminum foil. Place on grill and cook with lid closed for approximately 40 minutes. Serve with Cajun Butter.

Bryn's Mom's Butter Tarts

1	recipe pastry dough (see below), rolled and cut into tarts or 1 dozen frozen prepared tart shells	2 tbsp	corn syrup
1½	cups brown sugar	2 tbsp	half and half cream
2 tbsp	butter	½ tsp	vanilla
1	egg, lightly beaten	¾ cup	plump golden raisins
		¾ cup	toasted walnuts, coarsely chopped

Preheat oven to 400°F. Place prepared tart shells in refrigerator or freezer to chill for 10 minutes. In a large (4 cup) measuring cup, combine the brown sugar, butter and egg. Add corn syrup, cream and vanilla and mix well.

Into each tart shell, sprinkle ½ dozen raisins and a few walnut pieces. Pour enough of the filling into each shell to be ¾ full and bake for 25 minutes or until golden brown.

PASTRY DOUGH:

| 2 cups | unbleached all purpose flour | ¾ cup | vegetable shortening, divided |
| 1 tsp | salt | ¼ cup | cold water |

In a large mixing bowl, combine flour and salt. Using a pastry blender, cut in ½ cup shortening, and continue blending until the mixture resembles coarse cornmeal.

Add the remaining (¼ cup) shortening, and continue to blend and cut in until the crumbs are the size of peas. Sprinkle water over the flour mixture, and toss lightly with a fork.

Gather the dough into a ball. Roll out on a lightly floured surface and cut into an appropriate size to fit tart pans.

morning glory...

COFFEE

•

YOGURT AND GRANOLA
BREAKFAST PARFAITS

•

HUEVOS RANCHEROS

•

BACON TWO WAYS

SERVES 8

The sun has risen and it is time to get outdoors and embrace the day.
This satisfying breakfast will provide an energy boost that is sure to carry you through until lunch.
Best of all, it is portable so you can enjoy it at a leisurely pace on the dock with your cottage guests while you
soak up the sun and pour over the newspaper.

GETTING ORGANIZED

Up to three weeks before:
Make the Granola.

Up to one day ahead:
Make the tomato mixture for the Huevos Rancheros.

When you awake:
Make coffee, assemble parfaits, reheat tomato mix and poach eggs. Grill bacon,
and toast the tortillas on the upper rack.

Yogurt and Granola Breakfast Parfaits

1 cup	granola, see recipe below		3 cups	mixed berries: strawberries, raspberries and blueberries
2 cups	vanilla yogurt		½ cup	maple syrup

To assemble the parfaits, sprinkle a tablespoon of granola in the bottom of each parfait glass. Spoon in some yogurt, then fruit. Drizzle with maple syrup and top with more granola, and a single raspberry. Store leftover granola in an air tight container for up to 3 weeks.

BARBIE'S GRANOLA:

4 cups	old-fashioned rolled oats		½ cup	good quality honey
2 cups	sweetened coconut flakes		¾ cup	canola oil
2 cups	sliced almonds		1½ cups	dried apricots, diced
½ cup	sunflower seeds		1 cup	dried cherries
1 cup	roasted unsalted cashews		1 cup	dried cranberries

Mix the oats, coconut flakes and all the nuts and seeds in a large bowl.

In a small bowl mix together the honey and canola oil, and drizzle it over the oat mixture, mixing gently to combine.

Line 2 rimmed baking sheets with parchment paper. Spread the mixture over the 2 sheets and bake in a 350°F oven until golden brown, about 20 minutes. Let cool. Add the dried apricots, cherries and cranberries.

Place the amount you will need for a batch of parfaits in a small cast iron pan, and crisp it up on the barbecue for a few minutes before assembling.

Huevos Rancheros

1 tbsp	corn or canola oil		4	large tomatoes, seeded and chopped or 1 large can diced tomatoes, drained
1	small onion, chopped			salt and pepper, to taste
1	jalapeno pepper, seeded and minced		8	eggs
1	red pepper, seeded and chopped		8	flour tortillas
1 clove	garlic, minced			grated Monterey Jack or Cheddar cheese
1 tsp	cumin			cilantro, chopped
1 tbsp	mild chili powder			

In a large cast iron pan set over the side burner or on the barbecue on MEDIUM/LOW, heat oil and add onions and peppers. Cook, stirring, until softened. Add garlic, cumin and chili powder and saute 30 seconds before adding tomatoes. Continue cooking until tomatoes are soft, and the sauce begins to thicken. Season with salt and pepper.

Make 8 "wells" in the tomato mixture, and carefully crack an egg into each one. Cover the pan with a large lid, and cook until eggs are poached to desired doneness, about 5 minutes.

Meanwhile, lightly brush both sides of the tortillas with corn or canola oil. Lightly grill each side until heated.

To serve, place the tortilla on a heated plate. Scoop an egg and some tomato sauce onto the tortilla and garnish with shredded cheese and cilantro.

Bacon Two Ways

½ lb	side bacon strips		½ lb	sliced peameal bacon

Place side bacon strips on a pre-heated griddle, and back bacon directly on the grids. Cook both to your preference of crispness.

on the lighter side...

Grilled Tuna Salad Nicoise

•

Grilled Pineapple with
Mango Gelato

•

Fresh Fruit Platter

•

Limoncello Cocktails

Serves 8

Once in a blue moon when it is just you and your girlfriends at the cottage,
celebrate with this special treat – Limoncello cocktails and a meal that is no fuss, low in fat and scrumptious.

GETTING ORGANIZED

Up to one day ahead:
Make the vinaigrette, boil the eggs, blanch the green beans and make the glaze for the pineapple.

Up to one hour ahead:
Marinate the tuna and slice the onions, tomatoes and pineapple.
Preheat the grill, toss potatoes with olive oil and salt.

Immediately before serving:
Grill the potatoes for 30 minutes. Sear the tuna and assemble the salad.
Be sure to scrub the grids well with a wire brush before grilling the pineapple to avoid transferring any fish flavour.

Limoncello Cocktails

Limoncello
Champagne

You will need: Limoncello, well chilled in freezer and chilled champagne or sparkling white wine. Pour 1 ounce of Limoncello in the bottom of a champagne flute. Add 3 ounces champagne, and swirl to mix.

Grilled Tuna Salad Niçoise

4 small	tuna steaks		Vinaigrette:	
1½ tbsp	olive oil		3 tbsp	balsamic vinegar
3 tsp	lemon juice, freshly squeezed		1½ tbsp	lemon juice
	salt and pepper, to taste		8 tbsp	olive oil
24	mini potatoes, halved or quartered			salt and pepper, to taste
8	eggs, hard-boiled and halved		2 tsp	honey
1	red onion, thinly sliced		2 tsp	Dijon mustard
2	tomatoes, cut into 8 sections		Garnish:	
1 cup	green beans, stemmed and blanched		leafy green lettuce	
⅔ cup	Kalamata or Niçoise olives			

Marinate tuna steaks in olive oil and lemon juice for 1 hour. Sprinkle with salt and pepper.

Meanwhile, cook eggs for 10 minutes in gently boiling water and blanch green beans. Set aside in refrigerator.

Preheat the grill on MEDIUM for 10 minutes and brush the grids with vegetable oil.

Toss potatoes with olive oil and sprinkle with salt. Place on grill, cut side down, and cook, turning occasionally until tender, about 20 - 25 minutes. Set aside.

Place the tuna on the grids and cook according to the *guide for fish steaks, page18*, for a total of 8 minutes. *(Leave one area of the grids free so that they are clean and ready for grilling the pineapple spears.)*

Meanwhile, prepare Vinaigrette by combining balsamic vinegar, lemon juice, olive oil, salt, pepper, honey and mustard in a large glass jar. Shake vigorously.

To serve, arrange lettuce on plates and place potatoes, red onion, tomatoes and green beans in the centre of each plate. Arrange ½ tuna steak* on top of vegetables. Place eggs and olives attractively around the tuna and drizzle with Vinaigrette.

*NOTE: If serving for lunch, use ½ steak per person. Use whole steaks if serving as dinner.

Fresh Fruit Platter

Arrange your favourite fruits on a platter for healthy nibbling. Any kind of fruit will work well. Suggestions: Choose whatever is colourful and seasonal; Cherries, grapes, pineapple, raspberries, blueberries and peaches.

Grilled Pineapple with Mango Gelato

1	whole pineapple

Glaze:

3 tbsp	lemon juice
1 tbsp	honey
¼ tsp	cinnamon
500 g	tub Mango Gelato

Prepare pineapple by slicing lengthwise in quarters and removing core. Separate flesh from skin by carefully slicing along skin with a large, sharp knife. Cut pineapple flesh into spears. Combine lemon juice, honey and cinnamon in a small bowl.

Thoroughly clean and oil grids on free side of the barbecue. Arrange pineapple spears across grids and brush lightly with glaze. Cook for 4 minutes on MEDIUM. Turn, brush with glaze and cook for 4 - 5 minutes more.

Serve in a martini glass with a scoop of Mango gelato and garnish with mint leaves.

summer classics...

Sangria

•

California Quesadillas with Spicy Salsa
and Sour Cream

•

Summer Rolls with Shrimp and Mango

•

Grilled Caesar Salad

•

New York Strip Steaks
with Blue Cheese Compound Butter

•

Grilled Fingerling Potatoes

•

Composed Grilled Vegetable Platter

•

Old Fashioned Strawberry Shortcake

Serves 8

Summer calls for easy and relaxed entertaining, enjoying the freshness of the season. Welcome your guests with an icy glass of Sangria as they mingle and savour the spicy quesadillas and fresh summer rolls. To make this meal memorable, Caesar Salad gets a twist when you grill the baguette, bacon and even the romaine.
Finish off with a burst of summer-sweet strawberries in an old-fashioned favourite, shortcake.

GETTING ORGANIZED

Up to one week ahead:
Make the blue cheese compound butter and Caesar dressing.

Up to one day ahead:
Make the dipping sauce, and salsa, and bake the shortcake.

Up to 6 hours ahead:
Assemble the shrimp rolls and quesadillas, and grill the vegetables. Toss the strawberries with Grand Marnier and sugar.

As the night unfolds:
Grill the quesadillas, then the Caesar salad. Take a break from the table while you grill the steaks and potatoes.

Immediately before serving:
Prepare Crème Fraîche and assemble strawberry shortcake.

Sangria

1	bottle robust red wine		1	pint strawberries, hulled and diced
1	each of: lemon, lime and orange			

Slice lemon, lime and orange into rounds and place in large glass pitcher Add one 750 ml bottle full-bodied red wine and strawberries. Stir to mix, and let steep several hours if possible. To serve, fill a wine goblet with ice and add Sangria.

California Quesadillas with Spicy Salsa and Sour Cream

2	avocados, sliced		1 clove	garlic, minced
2 tbsp	lime juice, freshly squeezed		1 tsp	chili powder
2	tomatoes, seeded and chopped			salt and pepper, to taste
½	red onion, minced		¼ tsp	hot red pepper sauce
½	roasted red pepper, diced (See vegetable grilling guide, pg 20)		2 cups	smoked cheddar/Monterey Jack cheeses, grated
			6 - 12"	flour tortilla shells
¼ cup	cilantro, chopped		½ cup	sour cream

Slice avocado thinly and toss with lime juice. In a separate bowl, combine tomatoes, red onion, red pepper, cilantro, minced garlic, chili powder, hot sauce, salt and pepper and cheeses.

Preheat barbecue on MEDIUM for 10 minutes, reduce to LOW and lightly brush the grids with oil. Place 3 tortillas on a counter. Lay slices of avocado on tortillas. Spoon cheese mixture over top and spread evenly, leaving a ½" border. Cover with remaining tortillas.

Place tortillas directly on the cooking grids, and grill about 3 minutes per side, turning carefully using a large spatula. Transfer to a wooden cutting board and let rest for 3 - 5 minutes, before cutting into wedges with a large knife or pizza wheel.

Serve with Spicy Salsa and sour cream.

SPICY SALSA:

1	small red onion, chopped		4	jalapeño peppers, seeded and finely chopped
½ tsp	salt		4	medium tomatoes, chopped
	Juice of 2 limes		1 cup	chopped cilantro

Place the chopped onion in a bowl, sprinkle with the salt, squeeze the lime juice over, and set aside for 15 - 20 minutes. Add the chopped jalapeno peppers, tomatoes, and cilantro to the onion mixture, and stir. Serve immediately.

Grilled Fingerling Potatoes

3 lbs.	fingerling potatoes
	olive oil
	kosher salt

Scrub well. Toss with olive oil and kosher salt. Grill on MEDIUM 25 - 30 minutes, turning often.

Summer Rolls with Shrimp and Mango

16	rice paper wrappers		16	large shrimp, cooked, shelled and deveined, and halved lengthwise
2	heads boston bibb lettuce			
1	english cucumber, julienned		1	bunch mint sprigs, washed
4	green onions, julienned		1	bunch cilantro sprigs, washed
1	red bell pepper, julienned		½ cup	hoisin sauce
1	large mango, julienned			Sweet Chili Dipping Sauce (see recipe below)

Fill a wide, shallow dish with hot water. Working with 1 sheet of rice paper at a time, immerse in water and let stand until very pliable, for approximately 45 seconds. Remove from water and carefully arrange on a double layer of paper towels to drain.

Begin to assemble summer rolls by placing 2 halves of shrimp horizontally across the centre of the rice paper roll. Place a leaf of lettuce on top, trimmed to fit, leaving a 1" border on bottom edge and on each side. Top lettuce with 3-4 strips each of green onion, cucumber, red pepper, mango, and ½ teaspoon of hoisin sauce. Finish with a few sprigs each of cilantro and mint.

Roll up filling tightly in sheet, folding in 2 sides of sheet to completely enclose filling, and continue rolling. Transfer assembled rolls to a tray and cover with dampened paper towels. Repeat procedure with remaining rice paper sheets and filling ingredients. Tightly cover tray with plastic wrap (keeping dampened paper towels directly on spring rolls).

Spring rolls may be made 6 hours ahead and chilled. Just before serving cut spring rolls in half diagonally, with a serrated knife. Arrange spring rolls on a platter, garnish with cilantro sprigs and serve with Sweet Chili Dipping Sauce.

SWEET CHILI DIPPING SAUCE:

3 tbsp	fish sauce		2 tsp	brown sugar
3 tbsp	asian style sweet chili sauce		½	red hot chili, seeded and chopped (remove the seeds unless you like your sauce hot!)
1½ tbsp	lime juice			
1 tbsp	rice vinegar			

Combine all ingredients in a small bowl and stir to combine. Refrigerate until needed.

Composed Grilled Vegetable Platter

For the Vegetables:			*For the Topping*:	
2	zucchini, cut lengthwise		¼ lb	feta cheese, crumbled
2	yellow or orange peppers, cut in large chunks		¼ cup	Kalamata olives
½ lb	asparagus, blanched or grilled		*For the Basil Vinaigrette*:	
	olive oil		8 tbsp	olive oil
6	ripe tomatoes, cut in large chunks		5 tbsp	balsamic vinegar
				handful fresh basil, chopped
			2 cloves	garlic, minced

Lightly spray the zucchini and peppers with olive oil, and place on a preheated barbecue. Grill until tender crisp, turning 3 times. For *Perfect Grill Marks, see page 15 (see also the vegetable grilling guide, page 20)*. Once cooked, cut the peppers into strips. Whisk together the vinaigrette ingredients. On a large white platter, arrange the vegetables decoratively, with the tomatoes in the centre, the zucchini on the outside, the asparagus stacked against the zucchini, and the peppers stacked against the asparagus. Scatter the feta cheese and olives on top. Drizzle with Basil Vinaigrette.

Grilled Caesar Salad

⅓ cup	olive oil			salt and pepper, to taste
2 cloves	garlic, minced		8	thick slices peameal bacon
4	hearts of romaine lettuce, stems attached, halved lengthwise		1 cup	blender caesar salad dressing (see recipe below) chunk of parmesan Reggiano cheese, shaved
8	baguette slices		2	lemons, sliced into wedges

To infuse olive oil, heat olive oil in a small saucepan over LOW heat. Add garlic and cook until it sizzles and becomes very fragrant, about 1 minute. Remove from heat and add salt and pepper. Brush cut side of lettuce and both sides of the bread with the infused olive oil.

On a preheated, oiled grill, place the bacon, bread, lettuce (cut side down), and lemon wedges. Grill everything lightly, until grill marks appear, and lettuce is slightly wilted, approximately 3 minutes. Remove the lettuce to a platter, and continue to grill the bread and bacon on the second side.

To assemble: Place a romaine half on an individual dinner-size plate and drizzle with Blender Caesar Salad Dressing. Near the stem end place a piece of peameal bacon, and a slice of grilled baguette. Place parmesan shavings over top and garnish the plate with the grilled lemon wedge.

BLENDER CAESAR SALAD DRESSING:

4	medium garlic cloves, peeled		1 tsp	Worcestershire sauce
2	small cans anchovy filets		2 tsp	grainy Dijon mustard
2	large eggs		½ cup	parmesan cheese, grated
6 tbsp	balsamic vinegar			salt and freshly ground black pepper
3 tbsp	lemon juice		2½ cups	extra virgin olive oil

This recipe will make more than you need, but can be stored in a sealed jar in the refrigerator for a week.

With the metal blade fitted into a food processor, or blender, process garlic cloves until finely chopped. Add the anchovy filets and egg and continue processing for 30 seconds.

Add the balsamic vinegar, lemon juice, Worcestershire sauce, Dijon mustard and parmesan cheese, mixing until well blended. With the machine running, pour the olive oil slowly into the processor in a steady stream.

Dressing should become thick and creamy. Season with salt and pepper and add more parmesan cheese, if desired.

Grilled New York Strip Steaks with Blue Cheese Compound Butter

8-1½"	thick new york strip steaks		salt and freshly ground pepper, to taste

Bring steaks close to room temperature by removing them from the refrigerator ½ hour before cooking. Preheat barbecue on MEDIUM for 10 minutes and lightly oil the cooking grids.

Using our *Direct Grilling Guide, page 15*, follow the directions for *Grilling Perfect Steaks*. Place on heated plates and top with a disk of Blue Cheese Butter.

BLUE CHEESE COMPOUND BUTTER:

⅔ cup	butter, at room temperature	1 ½ tsp	fresh thyme leaves, finely chopped
⅓ cup	Roquefort cheese, crumbled		dash hot pepper sauce
1 tbsp	shallots, finely chopped		pinch salt

In a small bowl mix all ingredients together lightly with a fork until just evenly combined. Over mixing will cause it to become too blue in colour. Spoon the mixture onto a sheet of waxed paper, and shape it into a log about 1½" in diameter. Refrigerate 1 hour.

Slice into ⅓" thick rounds and place on hot Grilled New York Strip Steaks to melt. Freeze leftover butter pats.

Old Fashioned Strawberry Shortcake

1 cup	sugar	*For the strawberry topping*:	
¼ cup	butter, at room temperature	1 quart	strawberries, sliced
1	egg	3 tbsp	Grand Marnier
1 tsp	vanilla	2 tbsp	sugar
1 cup	milk, not quite full	*For the crème fraîche*:	
2 cups	unbleached flour	1 cup	whipping cream
	pinch salt	¼ cup	sour cream
2 tsp	baking powder	1 tsp	vanilla
		1 tbsp	sugar

Preheat oven to 350°F. Line a baking sheet with parchment paper. In a medium size bowl, beat together sugar and butter, add the egg and beat until light. Then add vanilla.

In a small bowl, combine flour, salt and baking powder, and gradually add flour mixture to the egg mixture, alternately with milk. Turn this thick, light batter out onto baking sheet and form into a round shape.

Bake about 25 minutes or until the colour of rice krispies.

Meanwhile slice the strawberries and sprinkle them with the Grand Marnier and 2 tablespoons of sugar. Toss lightly.

Just before serving, combine the whipping cream and sour cream in a medium bowl. Whip until soft peaks form, then add vanilla and 1 tbsp of sugar. Beat until just mixed.

To assemble: Slice cake in half and fill with half of crème fraîche and strawberries. Top with remaining crème fraîche and strawberries.

a harvest feast...

GRILLED FLATBREAD WITH
GOAT CHEESE AND HERBS

•

BEER CAN CHICKEN

•

GRILLED CORN SALAD

•

RATATOUILLE

•

PEACH COBBLER WITH
WHIPPED CREAM

SERVES 8

After a busy season of golfing, hiking and biking,
Labour Day is an appropriate occasion to relish the end of summer by
relaxing with your guests. Now is the time to enjoy late summers' bounty of herbs, veggies and peaches.
Toast the arrival of a new season as the days settle back into a different rhythm.

GETTING ORGANIZED

Up to one day ahead:
Make corn salad, omitting the fresh herbs, roast garlic for flatbread while grilling peppers for salad,
and toast pine nuts for flatbread.

The morning of:
Grill vegetables for ratatouille, cool and store in the refrigerator in a covered aluminum pan. Prepare cobbler and refrigerate
until ready to cook. Make dough for flatbread and refrigerate. Season the chicken with herbs, garlic and lemon.

Up to Two hours ahead:
Set up barbecue with drip pan under one side and pizza stone on the other.
Place chickens on the barbecue as directed in the recipe.

As the party unfolds:
Grill the flatbread and bake the cobbler.

Immediately before serving:
Add fresh herbs to the corn salad, and reheat ratatouille on the top rack of the grill for 15 minutes.
At the last minute, whip the cream for the cobbler.

Grilled Flatbread with Goat Cheese and Herbs

For the Dough:

1¼ tsp	active dry yeast
1 cup	lukewarm water
½ tsp	sugar
2 cups	unbleached flour
1 tbsp	olive oil
½ tsp	salt
1 tbsp	cornmeal

For the Topping:

1 head	garlic, roasted (see Vegetable Grilling Guide, page 20)
4 oz	goat cheese, crumbled
1 small	bunch fresh oregano, chopped
1 small	bunch fresh basil, chopped
1 small	bunch fresh parsley, chopped
1 cup	toasted pine nuts

To make flatbread dough, dissolve the yeast in lukewarm water with ½ teaspoon sugar. Add the flour, olive oil and salt and knead until elastic. Let rest 10 minutes before rolling. No rising is required.

If you have a pizza stone, place it on the grids on one side of the barbecue and preheat the barbecue on MEDIUM/HIGH, then reduce temperature to MEDIUM/LOW.

Shape dough by gently kneading and stretching thawed dough into desired shape, on a wooden pizza board or rimless baking tray, which has been liberally dusted with corn meal. Smear the roasted garlic over the dough, then scatter the remaining ingredients over top. Slide the flatbread onto the hot pizza stone, using a quick movement. Close the lid and cook approximately 10 minutes, or until the crust is crispy and cheese is warm.

NOTE: If you do not have a stone, oil a baking sheet, sprinkle with cornmeal and set the rolled dough on the baking sheet.

Grilled Corn Salad

8	cobs fresh corn
1	whole red pepper
1	whole yellow pepper
¼ cup	oil packed sun-dried tomatoes, chopped
1	jalapeno pepper, minced
2 tbsp	fresh chives, snipped
2 tbsp	cilantro, chopped

For the Vinaigrette:

1	small chipotle pepper (canned, in adobo sauce)
2 cloves	garlic, peeled
2 tbsp	red wine vinegar
1 tsp	frozen orange juice concentrate
½ cup	olive oil
	salt and pepper, to taste

Soak the corn cobs in their husks in a pail of cold water for 20 minutes. Meanwhile, preheat the barbecue on MEDIUM/HIGH, placing the red and yellow peppers directly on the grill. Turn the peppers occasionally, charring the skins on all sides. Remove the peppers to a cutting board. When cool enough to handle, peel the charred skin from the flesh; seed and chop. Set aside.

Reduce the heat to MEDIUM. Place the corn cobs on the barbecue, with their husks still on. Turn the cobs about every 5 minutes for a total of 20 minutes. Set aside until cool enough to handle, then peel and cut the niblets from the cobs with a sharp knife into a large bowl.

Add to this bowl the chopped red and yellow peppers, the sun-dried tomatoes, jalapeno pepper, chives and cilantro.

For the vinaigrette: In the bowl of a food processor* or in a blender, combine the chipotle peppers, garlic, vinegar and orange juice concentrate. Process for 20-30 seconds, then add the olive oil in a slow, steady stream, with the machine running. Add the salt and pepper to taste.

* If you do not have a food processor or a blender, finely mince the chipotle pepper and garlic, then add vinegar and orange juice. Slowly whisk in the olive oil. Drizzle the dressing over the vegetable mixture and serve.

NOTE: You may substitute 5-6 cups of thawed and drained frozen corn niblets when fresh corn is not in season. Can be made one day in advance, but do not add the chives and cilantro until just before serving.

Beer Can Chicken

1	large whole chicken (5 lbs)	1 sprig	fresh rosemary
1 355 ml	can of beer	1 sprig	fresh thyme
6 cloves	garlic, cut into thin slivers		salt and pepper, to taste
2	lemons, thinly sliced		

Prepare the chicken: Remove and discard the fat and giblets just inside the cavities of the chicken. Rinse and dry the chicken. Massage the breast and legs of the chicken to loosen the skin. Gently push your fingers between the skin and the meat, to create an opening and insert ⅔ of the garlic slivers, lemon slices and fresh rosemary and thyme. Season the outside of the chicken with freshly ground salt and pepper.

Prepare one side of the grill, as follows: Remove the grids and place a drip pan in the center of the barbecue. Replace the grids and brush with oil. Begin with liquid, beer or water in the drip pan.

Preheat on MEDIUM.

Pop the tab on the beer can and make several more large holes in the top of the can. Pour out the top inch of beer into the drip pan, then spoon any remaining garlic and herbs through the holes into the beer. As an alternative to beer, substitute 4 - 6 ounces of white wine, in a clean soup or pop can. Holding the chicken upright, with the opening of the body cavity down, insert the beer can into the cavity. Stand the chicken up in the center of the barbecue, over the drip pan. Spread out the legs to form a tripod, to support the chicken. The bird is now positioned with the wings at the top and the legs at the bottom, near the grids.

Close the grill and cook the chicken approximately 1½ hours, (18 minutes/pound), or until the internal temperature of the breast meat has reached 170°F. Beer will drip out of can during cooking. Continue to add more liquid to the drip pan as necessary so that it does not become dry. Place a carving tray on the shelf beside the barbecue and use tongs to lift the chicken, still containing the beer can, to the carving tray, holding a large metal spatula underneath the beer can for support. Let stand for 5 minutes before carving.

Ratatouille

1 small	eggplant, peeled and cut in thick slices		1 cup	cherry tomatoes, halved
3 tbsp	olive oil		1	red pepper, cut in large chunks
1 clove	garlic, minced		1	red onion, thickly sliced
1 tsp	fresh rosemary, chopped		1	zucchini, quartered lengthwise
½ tsp	kosher salt		2 tbsp	fresh oregano, chopped
4	tomatoes, stems removed, cut in half horizontally			salt and pepper, to taste

Sprinkle the eggplant slices with salt, and place them in a single layer between sheets of paper towels. Let drain for ½ hour.

Meanwhile, combine the olive oil, garlic, rosemary and salt in a flat-bottomed glass dish. Place in microwave oven for 20 seconds to infuse the oil with herb flavouring.

Gently loosen seeds in halved tomatoes and discard. Toss the cherry tomatoes, red pepper, red onion and zucchini in olive oil mixture, and add eggplant when ready. Add more olive oil if necessary.

Preheat barbecue on MEDIUM, placing a wok topper on one side. Reduce heat to MEDIUM/LOW, and brush the grids and wok topper with vegetable or olive oil.

Place the halved and cherry tomatoes in the wok topper, and tuck the remaining vegetables around the grill. When the tomatoes are cooked, move them to a cutting board. Transfer the eggplant and onions into the wok topper, and continue cooking as the vegetables caramelize in the residual tomato juices. Cook the peppers and zucchini until tender-crisp. Chop vegetables into uniform bite-sized pieces, sprinkle with oregano, salt and pepper and serve warm or at room temperature.

Peach Cobbler with Whipped Cream

For the Peach Filling:			2 tbsp	white sugar
8 cups	peaches, peeled and sliced		2 tsp	baking powder
½ cup	brown sugar		½ tsp	salt
2 tbsp	unbleached flour		⅓ cup	cold butter, cut into small pieces
½ tsp	cinnamon		⅓ cup	milk
1 tbsp	lemon juice		2 tbsp	heavy cream
4 tbsp	butter, melted		2 tbsp	white sugar, or as needed
For the Topping:			*For the Garnish*:	
1 cup	unbleached flour		1 cup	sweetened whipped cream

Preheat barbecue on MEDIUM. Adjust to maintain temperature at 350°F. Lightly grease a large, shallow oven proof baking dish or double layer of aluminum pans.

Combine peaches, brown sugar, flour, cinnamon, lemon juice and melted butter in a large bowl.

In a separate bowl, mix together 1 cup flour, 2 tablespoons white sugar, baking powder and salt. Cut in the cold butter with a pastry blender or 2 knives to form coarse crumbs. Sprinkle milk over the flour mixture and toss lightly with a fork until it just comes together.

Place the fruit mixture in the prepared pan, and top with mounds of the cobbler topping, leaving spaces in between. Brush with cream and sprinkle with remaining 2 tbsp white sugar.

Place the baking dish on the left side of the grill and turn off the left burner. Close the lid and bake 30 - 40 minutes, until the topping is lightly browned. Monitor the barbecue temperature while cooking and adjust as required to maintain 350°F. Serve garnished with a dollop of sweetened whipped cream.

gemütlichkeit...

Beer

•

Grilled Oktoberfest Sausage with
Spicy Mustard, Pickled Vegetables
and Fresh Pretzels

•

Boneless Pork Loin on the Rotisserie
with Beer Sauce and Sauerkraut

•

Hasselback Potatoes

•

Wilted Endive Salad with Bacon

•

Roasted Beet Salad

•

Apple Crisp

Serves 8

Gemütlichkeit defines Oktoberfest – the time of year when laughter rings and liveliness abounds as friends celebrate the harvest with each other. This fall menu is hearty with all the bounty of the season. It will also give you plenty of time to enjoy your Oktoberfest party. If it is a beautiful day, brush the leaves off the lawn furniture and set up outside.

GETTING ORGANIZED

Up to one day ahead:
Marinate the Pork Loin, prepare the Sauerkraut, make the Roasted Beet Salad (leaving off the feta),
cook the bacon and make the dressing for the Wilted Endive Salad.

The morning of your party:
Assemble and cook the Apple Crisp.

As the party unfolds:
One and a half hours ahead, start to rotisserie the roast and grill the potatoes. You should be able to leave
the grids on underneath the pork because it is a slender cut. Grill the sliced sausages, briefly heat the fresh pretzels wrapped in
foil, and assemble the appetizer platter.

Immediately before serving:
Once the meat is cooked, let it rest, covered with foil, while you reduce the beer marinade. Reheat the vinaigrette in the
microwave and toss the salads, garnishing the beet salad with the feta cheese. Reheat the Apple Crisp on the grill or in the oven.

Grilled Oktoberfest Sausage with Spicy Mustard, Pickled Vegetables and Fresh Pretzels

1 lb	Oktoberfest Sausage, a smoked bratwurst sausage		assortment of pickled vegetables,
8	fresh pretzels, purchased at a German bakery		such as dill pickles, pickled onions,
	jar of spicy smoked mustard		and pickled baby corns

Oktoberfest sausage is smoked, thus needing only quick grilling to prepare. Simply cut the sausages into ½ inch thick pieces, slicing on the diagonal. Preheat barbecue on MEDIUM, place sausage directly on the grids, and cook 3 minutes per side.

Heat pretzels by wrapping in foil and placing them on the upper rack of the barbecue for 2 minutes, to heat through. Serve sausage on a platter with warm pretzels, spicy smoked mustard and an assortment of pickled vegetables.

Boneless Pork Loin on the Rotisserie with Beer Sauce & Sauerkraut

4 lb	boneless pork loin		3 cups	beer
½ cup	Dijon mustard		2 tbsp	vegetable oil
1	medium onion, finely chopped			salt and freshly ground black pepper
½ cup	honey			

In a large saucepan, stir together the mustard, onion, honey, beer and vegetable oil. Bring marinade just to a boil, stirring, and remove from heat. Let cool to room temperature.

Sprinkle pork loin with salt and pepper. Place meat in a large, resealable plastic bag or in a glass dish large enough to hold it. Pour in ½ of the marinade turning occassionaly. Refrigerate at least 8 or up to 24 hours. Let stand at room temperature for 40 minutes before barbecuing.

Set up the barbecue for rotisserie cooking, placing a drip pan below. Heat barbecue to about 400°F, and place the pork on the spit in the barbecue.*

Reduce heat to MEDIUM LOW, about 375°F. Cook about 1½ hours, until it is golden brown and the internal temperature reaches 155°F.

Let rest, tented with foil on a platter about 20 minutes. Meanwhile, place the pan of prepared sauerkraut on the grill to heat through. Bring remaining marinade to a boil, and reduce slightly, about 5 minutes.

To serve: Spoon sauerkraut around the pork, and pour the reduced marinade over top.

Refer to page 23 for instructions on rotisserie set up.

SAUERKRAUT:

1	large bag Sauerkraut, (or 2 tins depending on availability)		1	tart apple, peeled and sliced
1 tbsp	olive oil		1 tsp	caraway seeds, crushed
1	onion, sliced			salt and pepper, to taste

Drain and rinse sauerkraut lightly. In a large sauté pan equipped with a lid, heat olive oil over medium low heat on the side burner or stovetop. Add onions, and cook until translucent, about 5 minutes. Add apple slices, and continue cooking until apples are slightly softened.

Add sauerkraut, caraway seeds, salt and pepper. Cover with lid. Heat for 20 minutes, or until warmed through.

Hasselback Potatoes

| 8 | medium potatoes, Yukon Gold | 3 tbsp | olive oil |
| 2 | small onions, sliced thinly | | salt and pepper, to taste |

Preheat grill on MEDIUM for 5 minutes. Prepare potatoes by scrubbing to clean outside skin. Slice potatoes 10-12 times, ¾ way through, leaving skin intact, to create a fan. Insert onion slices into spaces created in potatoes. Brush with olive oil and season with salt and pepper. Wrap individually in foil, place on grill and cook for 40 minutes.

Wilted Endive Salad with Bacon

2	small heads curly endive, or other bitter greens	⅓ cup	white wine vinegar
1	small head radicchio, shredded	1 tsp	Dijon mustard
5 slices	bacon, cut into 1" pieces		salt and freshly ground black pepper, to taste
⅓ cup	white sugar		

Place lettuce in a large bowl. Fry the bacon in a heavy skillet over medium heat, until crisp. Remove from skillet with a slotted spoon, and toss over the greens. Add sugar, vinegar, mustard and salt and pepper to the skillet. Swirl to blend and simmer until the sugar is dissolved. Pour over the lettuce and toss lightly.

Roasted Beet Salad

8	medium beets, scrubbed and halved	¼ cup	walnut oil
	olive oil		salt and pepper, to taste
2 tbsp	onion, finely chopped	¼ cup	crumbled feta cheese
2 tbsp	raspberry vinegar	2 tbsp	fresh parsley, finely chopped

Using 2 large sheets of heavy duty aluminum foil, lay 4 beets on top of each sheet. Drizzle beets with olive oil, and wrap the foil around them in a package, taking care to seal the edges well. Place them on the upper rack of a preheated barbecue or in the oven at 350°F and roast until tender, approximately an hour. Let cool and peel if desired. Cut into large dice.

In a large bowl, combine the vinegar, walnut oil, salt and pepper and taste to adjust. The sweetness of the beets will come through, so a sour vinaigrette works well. Toss in the prepared beets and onion. Can be prepared a day or two ahead up to this point. Just before serving, top with crumbled feta and chopped parsley. Serve at room temperature.

Apple Crisp

For the Filling:		½ cup	packed brown sugar
7-8	medium cooking apples, peeled and sliced	½ cup	all-purpose flour
2 tbsp	sugar	½ cup	rolled oats
½ tsp	cinnamon	1 tsp	cinnamon
For the Topping:			pinch salt
5 tbsp	cold butter, cut into pieces	½ cup	finely chopped pecans or ground almonds

Preheat oven to 350°F. Butter an 8" square baking dish. Prepare the apples, and toss them with sugar and cinnamon. Spread the mixture evenly in the buttered dish.

For the topping: Combine the butter, sugar, flour, oats, cinnamon and salt in a medium size bowl. Work together with fingertips or cut with a pastry blender until the mixture resembles coarse meal. Toss in nuts.

Sprinkle half the topping over the apples. Bake 30 minutes, then sprinkle remaining topping over top. Bake another 30 minutes, until bubbly and until the apples are tender. Serve warm with vanilla ice cream.

autumn bounty...

HOT APPLE CIDER

•

ROASTED RED PEPPER CROSTINI

•

SPINACH SALAD WITH
POMEGRANATE VINAIGRETTE

•

ROTISSERIE CHICKENS WITH
MEDITERRANEAN FLAVOURS

•

STUFFED ACORN SQUASH

•

STEAMED BROCCOLI

•

SAVOURY MASHED
POTATO CASSEROLE

•

PUMPKIN PIE WITH
WHIPPED CREAM

SERVES 8

Thanksgiving is the highly-anticipated family gathering with all of your favourite fall foods.
The warmth of the occasion is reflected in the cornucopia of sweet and savoury vegetables.
This meal comes with a tempting twist – moist and crispy rotisserie chickens. When the tasty vegetables and hot
apple cider are finished, there is still no substitute for that traditional slice of mouth-watering pumpkin pie.

GETTING ORGANIZED

Up to one day ahead:
Prepare Pumpkin Pie, Savoury Mashed Potato Casserole, vinaigrette for Spinach Salad, Acorn Squash and its stuffing.
Toast baguettes, roast the red peppers and prepare garlicky cheese spread for the Crostini.
Marinate the chickens.

Two hours ahead:
Set up rotisserie and cook chickens.

As the night unfolds:
Reheat potatoes and squash, assemble, heat and serve crostini.

Immediately before serving:
Prepare Spinach Salad and steam broccoli. Whip the cream in time for dessert.

Roasted Red Pepper Crostini

1	large baguette, thinly sliced		1	large, roasted red pepper (See page 20), sliced
½ lb	cream cheese or chèvre		½ cup	pesto sauce (See page 157), or store bought
1	head roasted garlic (See Vegetable Grilling Guide, page 20)			

To make toast rounds: Spray both sides of sliced baguette with olive oil. Place on grids of preheated barbecue and toast until golden brown, turning once. Can be stored in a sealed container for up to 3 days.

To prepare garlicky cheese spread: Blend roasted garlic and softened cheese in a glass bowl. Set aside until ready to use. Can be refrigerated for up to a week.

To Assemble Crostini: Spread toast rounds with a heaping teaspoon of garlicky cheese spread. Top with 2 - 3 slices of roasted red pepper and a dollop of pesto. Place on upper rack of barbecue and warm until cheese is soft and bubbly. Serve immediately.

Spinach Salad with Pomegranate Vinaigrette

8 cups	baby spinach leaves		*Vinaigrette*:	
1 cup	cherry tomatoes		10 tbsp	canola oil
½	red onion, thinly sliced		4 tbsp	pomegranate vinegar
½ cup	pumpkin seeds, roasted		1 tsp	honey
½ cup	dried cranberries, substitute pomegranate seeds, if available		½ tsp	salt

Prepare vinaigrette by combining canola oil, pomegranate vinegar, honey and salt in a resealable glass jar. Shake vigorously.

In a large glass bowl, toss spinach, cherry tomatoes and red onion in a large glass bowl, with vinaigrette. Top with pumpkin seeds and dried cranberries.

Savoury Mashed Potato Casserole

12	large russet potatoes, peeled and quartered		½ tsp	salt
4	green onions, chopped		¼ tsp	white pepper
½ lb	cream cheese		2 tbsp	butter
2 cups	light sour cream		1 cup	parmesan cheese, freshly grated

Place peeled potatoes in a large pot and cover with cool, salted water. Cover and bring to a boil, reduce heat to MEDIUM and continue cooking until tender, approximately 30 minutes.

Meanwhile, chop green onions, and combine with cream cheese, sour cream, salt and pepper.

Drain potatoes, place into a large mixing bowl with butter and mash with a potato masher. Add cream cheese mixture and beat with an electric mixer until fluffy.

Spoon mixture into a buttered aluminum tray or pan and sprinkle with Parmesan cheese. Can be refrigerated overnight at this point, covered tightly.

Place in an oven or barbecue, preheated to 350°F and bake, uncovered, until golden brown, approximately 40-50 minutes.

NOTE: Can be prepared up to 2 days in advance and heated in the barbecue or oven, when needed.

Rotisserie Chicken with Mediterranean Flavours

2	5 lb chickens, whole, giblets and neck removed	¼ cup	fresh parsley, chopped
¼ cup	olive oil	1 tsp	crushed red pepper
2	whole lemons, quartered	10 cloves	garlic, sliced
¼ cup	fresh thyme, chopped	2	whole cooking onions, quartered
¼ cup	fresh rosemary, chopped		

Rinse chickens with cold water; pat dry with paper towels. To prepare chickens for marinade, gently massage skin over breast and leg areas to loosen skin from the flesh. This will create a pocket between the skin and flesh.

Combine olive oil, juice of one lemon and fresh herbs and crushed red pepper in a glass measuring cup. Gently lift skin and pour olive oil and fresh herb mixture into the pockets. Massage into breast and leg meat.

Insert 6 sliced garlic cloves in various areas under the skin.

Stuff remaining lemon quarters, onion and garlic cloves into the cavities of the birds. Generously sprinkle salt and pepper over outside of chickens.

Truss the chickens tightly with cotton string. Place in resealable plastic bags and marinate in the refrigerator for at least 4 hours, or overnight.

Rotisserie method:

Arrange your barbecue as appropriate for the size of the chickens, removing grids and warming racks if necessary, and placing a drip pan on the vapourizer. Position drip pan so that it will be centred below the chickens. Fill the drip pan to ½" from the top with water, wine or fruit juice. Preheat the barbecue on MEDIUM for 10 minutes.

To place chickens on the rotisserie, slide one of the skewer forks onto the spit, insert the spit rod into the centre of the bird, lengthwise, then dovetail the second chicken. Centre the chickens on the spit and secure them in place with the remaining fork. Tighten the forks securely. Check that they are balanced and reposition spit rod if necessary. Position the counterbalance for even rotation. To do this, lay the rod with the chickens over the kitchen sink allowing the heaviest side to turn to the bottom. With the counterbalance loosened, rotate it to the opposite side, facing up. Tighten the rod handle.

Set the rotisserie rod in the slots of the barbecue casting. Keep an eye on the heat indicator on the lid of the barbecue and try to keep the temperature around 375ºF. Check periodically to ensure that the drip pan does not run dry. Keep a pitcher of hot water handy, to refill the drip pan as it begins to evaporate.

Cook the chickens indirectly over MEDIUM heat for approximately 1½ hours, until the juices run clear, or 15 - 20 minutes per pound. The only way to accurately tell when the chicken is done is to use a meat thermometer. Do not allow the thermometer to touch the bone or the rotisserie spit. Chicken is done when the internal temperature of the breast meat has reached 170ºF and the legs 180ºF. If using a rear rotisserie burner, you may need to also set the lower burners on LOW depending on winds, external temperature etc.

Convection method: *Refer to page 23* for complete instructions for setting up your grill for rotisserie cooking, or for options if your grill is not equipped with a rotisserie.

Let chickens stand for at least 10 minutes before carving.

Stuffed Acorn Squash

4	acorn squash		½	onion, diced
For the stuffing:			1 tsp	olive oil
1	parsnip, peeled and cut into ½" cubes		1 tbsp	apple cider
1	carrot, peeled and cut into ½" cubes		2 tbsp	pumpkin seeds
1	sweet potato, peeled and cut into ½" cubes			salt and pepper, to taste
1	cob of corn, kernels removed			maple syrup
1 clove	garlic, minced			

For the stuffing: Preheat barbecue to MEDIUM. Spray large piece of aluminum foil with vegetable oil spray. Place parsnip, carrot, sweet potato, corn, garlic and onion in middle of foil, and toss with olive oil and apple cider. Fold foil into pouch. Place on grids, reduce heat to MEDIUM/LOW and cook for 35 minutes. Remove from heat and set aside.

Acorn squash: Cut in half lengthwise and remove seeds. Rub inside with butter and season with salt and pepper. Place on grids, cut side up, and cook for 35 minutes, until tender.

If serving immediately: Assemble stuffed acorn squash by placing a scoop of stuffing into each acorn squash half, and top with pumpkin seeds and maple syrup.

If serving the next day: Store covered, in the refrigerator. Assemble stuffed acorn squash by placing a scoop of stuffing into each half of acorn squash and reheat on the barbecue for 20 minutes on MEDIUM. Top with pumpkin seeds and drizzle with maple syrup before serving.

Pumpkin Pie with Whipped Cream

For the Pastry:			½ tsp	salt
2 cups	unbleached all purpose flour		1 tsp	cinnamon
1 tsp	salt		½ tsp	ground ginger
¾ cup	vegetable shortening, divided		¼ tsp	ground nutmeg
¼ cup	cold water		⅛ tsp	ground allspice
For the Pumpkin Filling:			⅛ tsp	ground cloves
2 cups	canned pumpkin		dash	mace
1½ cups	whipping cream		2	eggs, slightly beaten
¼ cup	brown sugar		*For Garnish*:	
½ cup	white sugar		1 cup	sweetened whipped cream

Preheat oven to 425ºF.

In a large mixing bowl, combine flour and salt. Using a pastry blender, cut in ½ cup shortening, and continue blending until the mixture resembles coarse cornmeal. Add the remaining shortening, and continue to blend and cut in until the crumbs are the size of peas. Sprinkle water over the flour mixture, and toss lightly with a fork. Gather the dough into a ball, and divide into two.

Shape into disks, wrap, and freeze one half for later, if desired. Roll the other disk on a lightly floured surface. Lay a 9" pie plate over the rolled dough and cut a 1" border around the edge. Remove pie plate, gently lift one corner of the dough, and carefully fold loosely in half, without breaking it in the centre. Lift and place the pastry in the pie plate, trying not to stretch it to fit. Crimp the edges decoratively with your fingers.

Mix all the filling ingredients in a large bowl, and pour into the pie shell. Bake 15 minutes at 425ºF, then reduce heat to 350ºF and bake about 45 minutes longer. Cool on a wire rack. Garnish with whipped cream.

comfort & joy...

CRANBERRY GIN AND TONICS

•

SWEET ROSEMARY BAR NUTS

•

CAPICOLLA AND ASIAGO PINWHEELS

•

SWEET POTATO SOUP WITH
CRISPY SAGE AND STILTON

•

TURKEY WITH CORNBREAD STUFFING

•

CRANBERRY SAUCE

•

GARLIC MASHED POTATOES

•

CARROTS WITH ORANGE MAPLE GLAZE

•

SHREDDED BRUSSELS SPROUTS
WITH PANCETTA AND PINE NUTS

•

MINCEMEAT PIE WITH HARD SAUCE

SERVES 8

This colourful holiday dinner serves up a delicious feast for your family to savour. With the Christmas turkey on the barbecue, your oven is free for cooking appetizers and extra stuffing, and for baking or reheating the pie. Once the turkey is on the grill it will need little attention. Simply check the drip pan periodically and add hot liquid when necessary. Enhance the spirit of giving and sharing by inviting others to help with the rest of the preparations in the kitchen.

GETTING ORGANIZED

Up to a week ahead:
Make the cornbread, cranberry sauce, hard sauce, mincemeat pie and nuts.
The sauces will keep in the refrigerator, but play it safe and put the rest into the freezer.

Up to 2 days ahead:
Make the syrup for the gin and tonics, prepare the sweet potato soup, roll the pinwheels and combine the stuffing ingredients.

Christmas Day:
While the turkey is on the barbecue, recruit your family to pitch in with the appetizers and vegetables.
Peel and prepare the potatoes. Slice and bake the appetizers. Crisp the sage.

Immediately before serving:
Cook the carrots and brussels sprouts. Reheat the pie as you sit down to dinner.

Cranberry Gin & Tonics

1	12 oz bag cranberries		6 cups	chilled tonic water
½ cup	sugar		1¼ cups	gin
¼ cup	water		¼ cup	plus 1 tsp fresh lime juice

Bring cranberries, sugar, and water to a simmer in a 3 quart saucepan. Simmer, uncovered, stirring occasionally until berries just begin to pop, about 2 minutes.

Drain cranberries in a fine-mesh sieve set over a 1 quart glass measuring cup. Reserve ½ cup cranberries and force remaining berries through sieve into syrup. Discard solids remaining in sieve, then add reserved cranberries to syrup. Cool to room temperature.

Transfer to a pitcher and chill until cold, about 2 hours. Syrup can be made 2 days ahead and chilled, covered.

Add tonic water, gin, and lime juice just before serving.

Sweet Rosemary Bar Nuts

1¼ lbs	assorted raw nuts		2 tsp	dark brown sugar
2 tbsp	fresh rosemary, coarsely chopped		2 tsp	kosher salt
½ tsp	cayenne		1 tbsp	butter, melted

Preheat oven to 350°F. In a large bowl, toss nuts with the remaining ingredients and spread them on a rimmed cookie sheet. Toast in the oven until they turn golden in colour, stirring occasionally, about 15-20 minutes. When cooled completely, store in an airtight container.

Capicolla and Asiago Pinwheels

1½	cups grated Asiago cheese		2 tsp	Dijon mustard
2 tsp	fresh thyme, chopped		24 slices	capicolla ham, 1½" diameter
2 tbsp	fresh oregano, chopped		1	large egg, beaten
1	frozen puff pastry sheet, thawed			non-stick vegetable oil cooking spray

Preheat oven to 400°F.

Mix the cheese and herbs together in a bowl. Lay out the puff pastry sheet and cut into 2 rectangles. Spread Dijon mustard on one side of each rectangle, being sure to leave a 1" border on one long edge. Place half the ham, and sprinkle half of the cheese over each rectangle. Brush the border with egg wash, then roll the pastry up starting at the side opposite the egg-washed one. Repeat with the other rectangle. Wrap the rolls in plastic wrap and chill, seam side down, for at least 30 minutes or up to 24 hours.

When ready to bake, line 2 baking sheets with parchment paper. Place the roll on a cutting board, seam side down. Slice into ¼" thick rounds. Brush the pinwheels with egg wash. Bake on the middle rack until golden brown, approximately 15 minutes.

Sweet Potato Soup with Crispy Sage and Stilton

5	large sweet potatoes		3 tbsp	butter
2	russet potatoes		5 cups	chicken broth
¾ cup	onion, finely chopped		¾ cup	dry white wine
2	leeks, cleaned and chopped		5½ cups	water
2	large garlic cloves, minced		1	bunch, sage
3	large carrots, sliced thin		8 oz	Stilton cheese, crumbled
1	bay leaf			

No need to waste precious minutes peeling potatoes! Scrub and pierce the sweet potatoes and russet potatoes and place them on the barbecue early in the day. Roast potatoes on MEDIUM for 45-50 minutes. Let cool for 15 minutes, then simply scoop out the flesh, for use in the soup later.

When you have 15 minutes of free time, complete the soup! In a stock pot, melt butter and add the onion, leek, garlic, carrots and bay leaf. Cook over low heat, stirring until the vegetables have softened.

Add the chicken broth, wine and water and simmer, covered, for 15 minutes. Add the flesh of the sweet potatoes and russet potatoes and simmer 10 minutes, discard the bay leaf. In a blender, puree the soup in batches, until it is very smooth. Season the soup with salt and pepper. This soup may be made a day or 2 in advance. Thin with additional stock, or water, as required.

To make crispy sage garnish: Heat 3 tbsp of oil in a frying pan. When oil begins to sizzle, gently drop in clean and dry sage leaves and allow to fry for 1-2 minutes. Remove carefully and let cool on a paper towel. Sprinkle with coarse sea salt.

Serve soup in individual wide mouthed bowls, topping each with a crispy sage leaf and a tablespoon of Stilton cheese.

Turkey with Cornbread Stuffing

For the Stuffing:			4 cups	onion, chopped
1	recipe Simple Cornbread, (see page 68)		1½ cups	celery, chopped
	(no need to grill the squares for this recipe)		10	oil packed sun-dried tomatoes, chopped
1 tbsp	olive oil		½ cup	fresh parsley, chopped
¾ lb	hot Italian sausage, casings removed, crumbled		1	15 lb turkey, rinsed and patted dry

Prepare Simple Cornbread according to the recipe (page 68) and let cool. Crumble or cut into small squares and set aside in a large bowl.

Meanwhile, heat the olive oil in a large sauté pan and add the crumbled sausage. Cook until browned, then add the onion and celery, stirring until translucent. Add sausage and vegetables to the cornbread as well as the sun-dried tomatoes and parsley. Toss to combine.

Lightly stuff the cavity of the turkey and truss the bird, being sure to tuck the wings underneath. Place the remaining stuffing in a covered, greased casserole dish and heat through at 350°F for 25 - 30 minutes.

Place a drip pan below the grids and fill halfway with hot water and wine or cranberry juice as desired. Preheat the barbecue on MEDIUM, then reduce temperature to MEDIUM/LOW and brush or spray the grids with olive oil.

Place the turkey on the barbecue and close the lid. As a general rule, count on 15 minutes per pound, but be sure to use a meat thermometer to determine doneness, testing after about 3 hours.

*Breast meat should be cooked to 170ºF, and dark meat to 180ºF.

* Winds and weather can affect the cooking time so factor sub-zero temperatures into your calculations! Continue to monitor the level of the liquid in the drip pan and never let it completely dry as this can result in a flare-up. When necessary, pour in more hot water, being sure to wear an oven mitt to avoid steam burns.

Cranberry Sauce

3 cups	fresh or frozen whole cranberries	1 cup	water
1 cup	white sugar	1 tbsp	lemon or orange zest, grated

Rinse cranberries and set aside. In a medium saucepan combine sugar and water. Bring to a boil and add lemon zest. Boil 5 minutes. Add cranberries, return to a boil, reduce heat and simmer gently until the skins pop, about 5 minutes. Remove from heat and refrigerate. Can be made up to a week ahead.

Garlic Mashed Potatoes

6-8	large Yukon gold or baking potatoes, peeled and halved	⅔ cup	milk (more or less as required), heated
1	head garlic, divided and peeled		salt and pepper, to taste
¼ cup	butter, at room temperature		

Place potatoes, garlic and 1 tbsp of salt in a large pot and cover by 1" with cold water. Bring to a boil over HIGH heat, then reduce the temperature and simmer gently until the potatoes are very tender.

Drain thoroughly in a colander, then return to the pot and place over a low flame to dry the potatoes slightly (about 1 minute). Add the butter and mash the potatoes and garlic with a masher. Add milk to the desired consistency. Season generously with salt and pepper.

To hold mashed potatoes made in advance, place them in a heat-proof bowl, sealed tightly with foil, over gently simmering water.

Shredded Brussels Sprouts with Pancetta and Pine Nuts

2 lbs	brussels sprouts, trimmed of cores	2 tbsp	fresh lemon juice
2 tbsp	olive oil		salt and freshly ground pepper, to taste
2 cloves	garlic, minced	½ cup	toasted pine nuts
6 slices	pancetta, roughly chopped		fresh parmesan cheese, shaved

Cut trimmed brussels sprouts in half, then thinly slice. Set aside.

In a large skillet heat olive oil on MEDIUM HIGH. Add pancetta and sauté until fat begins to render and pancetta begins to brown. Add garlic and brussels sprouts, toss well to coat, and continue to sauté another few minutes. Cover to steam until tender-crisp.

Season with salt and pepper, add lemon juice and sprinkle with toasted pine nuts.

Serve with shavings of parmesan cheese.

Carrots with Orange Maple Glaze

3 lbs	carrots, peeled		1 tbsp	orange juice
2 tbsp	butter		1 tsp	ginger root, peeled and grated
2 tbsp	maple syrup			salt and pepper, to taste

Steam whole carrots for 4 minutes. Meanwhile, prepare glaze by melting butter in a large sauté pan. Add maple syrup, orange juice and grated ginger. When butter is melted, add steamed carrots and sauté gently for 4 minutes. Season with salt and pepper.

Mincemeat Pie with Hard Sauce

1	recipe for pastry (See page 95)		1	jar Crosse & Blackwell Mincemeat Pie Filling

To make Mincemeat Pie, follow pastry instructions for Pumpkin Pie Pastry, (page 95), using all of the pastry for a double crust pie.

Fill with prepared mincemeat. Roll out top crust, lay it over the filling and pinch edges together decoratively. Cut a small steam vent "x" in the centre.

Bake at 425°F for 15 minutes, until beginning to brown, then reduce temperature to 350°F and bake 30 minutes more. Remove from oven and let cool.

HARD SAUCE:

1¼ cups	icing sugar, sifted		2 tbsp	sherry
⅓ cup	butter, at room temperature			pinch salt

Blend all ingredients with a spoon until smooth.

Can be made 3 days in advance of serving and refrigerated. Bring back to room temperature one hour before serving. Place a small scoop along side each slice of mincemeat pie.

embracing the elements...

GRILLED MINESTRONE SOUP

•

CARAMELIZED ONION AND
GOAT CHEESE SPREAD

•

GARLIC BREAD

•

SWEET MARIE BARS

•

HOT CHOCOLATE

SERVES 8

When the party is outside, you want to be where the fun is. It does not get any easier than when kids and adults can enjoy a satisfying meal together at rinkside.

Take the chill off with a steamy meal-in-a-bowl: warming soup and creamy hot chocolate.

GETTING ORGANIZED

One day ahead:
Make the soup, caramelized onion spread and Sweet Marie Bars.

The morning of:
Prepare the hot chocolate and store in a large thermos.

Immediately before serving:
Simply reheat the soup and Caramelized Onion and Goat Cheese Spread.
Only the garlic bread requires last-minute grilling.

Grilled Minestrone Soup

This is a great way to use up any left over grilled vegetables and sausages. If the tomatoes in your grocery store have the winter blahs, substitute a 28 ounce tin of tomatoes. For a vegetarian alternative, omit the sausage and substitute vegetable broth for the chicken stock.

1 doz	plum tomatoes, halved		12 cups	chicken stock
2	carrots, peeled and sliced lengthwise		3 cloves	garlic, peeled and minced
1	zucchini, sliced lengthwise		1	bay leaf
1	small eggplant, peeled and sliced lengthwise		1 can	kidney beans
1	red bell pepper, cut in large chunks		1	small bunch fresh basil, chopped
1	large onion, peeled and sliced thickly		1	small bunch fresh oregano, chopped
3 tbsp	olive oil		1/3 cup	parmesan cheese, grated
4	Italian sausages			
¾ cup	macaroni pasta, cooked according to package directions until al dente			

Slice tomatoes in half and gently remove the seeds with your fingers. Sprinkle tomatoes with salt and place cut side down on paper towels to drain for ½ hour.

Preheat barbecue on MEDIUM.

Prepare carrots, zucchini, eggplant, red pepper and onion as directed above and toss all vegetables with olive oil.

Meanwhile, cook pasta according to package directions, drain and rinse with cold water, and set aside.

Reduce barbecue heat to MEDIUM/LOW and place the sausages and all the vegetables except the garlic on the grill, and cook until vegetables are starting to soften. The vegetables will continue to soften in the soup, so they do not need to be completely cooked through. Meanwhile, bring stock to a boil in a large pot on the sideburner of the barbecue or on the stove. Add the minced garlic, oregano and bay leaf, and reduce heat to a simmer.

Transfer the grilled vegetables and sausage to a cutting board, and dice vegetables into bite-size pieces. You may want to remove the tomato skins before dicing them. Slice the sausages into ¼" pieces, and add everything to the chicken stock. Simmer until the vegetables are soft and flavours are nicely combined, about 25 minutes. Add the cooked pasta and drained beans and simmer for another 5 minutes to heat through. Add the chopped basil and oregano, season with salt and pepper and simmer for another minute.

Serve steaming hot in warmed bowls, and sprinkle with parmesan cheese, if desired.

Garlic Bread

Golden brown and crunchy on the outside, tender and moist on the inside, garlic bread is also a great accompaniment to chicken salad, steak, or pasta.

8	thick slices Italian bread		3 tbsp	olive oil
3 tbsp	salted butter		2	large cloves garlic, minced

Place butter, oil, and garlic in a small bowl. Cover loosely with plastic wrap, and microwave on high 25 seconds until butter is melted and garlic flavour is infused. Brush both sides of the bread with the butter mixture. Grill on MEDIUM-LOW until golden brown, turning to create Perfect Grill Marks *(refer to page 15)*.

Caramelized Onion and Goat Cheese Spread

2	onions, thickly sliced	2	small logs of goat cheese
1 tbsp	olive oil	2 tbsp	balsamic vinegar
1 tbsp	butter	2 tbsp	chopped fresh basil
1	head garlic		

In a large skillet over MEDIUM heat, combine olive oil and butter. When melted and sizzling slightly, add onions and toss to coat. Cook for 5 minutes, stirring the onions occasionally, and reduce the temperature to LOW, continue cooking until the onions are very soft and golden brown. This can take up to 40 minutes. Your patience is worth it!

Meanwhile, place the garlic head on a square of aluminum foil. Drizzle with olive oil, wrap tightly and place in a 400°F oven or barbecue MEDIUM/LOW for 30 minutes, until softened. Let cool.

When the garlic is cool enough to handle, squeeze the roasted garlic cloves into the onions. Roughly cut up the goat cheese and add it to the onion mixture.

Place on the upper rack of the barbecue while toasting garlic bread, until bubbling, for approximately 10-15 minutes (or place in a 350°F oven). Remove from heat and stir in the vinegar and basil. Serve with garlic bread.

Sweet Marie Squares

½ cup	brown sugar, packed	**For the Topping:**	
½ cup	chocolate chips	1 cup	chocolate chips
½ cup	peanut butter	1 tbsp	peanut butter
½ cup	corn syrup		
1 tbsp	butter		
2 cups	rice krispies		

Lightly butter an 8" x 8" pan. In a large glass bowl, combine brown sugar, ½ cup chocolate chips, ½ cup peanut butter, corn syrup, and butter. Microwave on HIGH for 1½ minutes, then stir until melted. Add the rice krispies, stir to combine, then turn out into prepared square pan. Pack down until level.

In a small glass bowl, combine 1 cup chocolate chips with 1 tbsp peanut butter. Microwave on HIGH for 1 minute and stir until melted and smooth. Pour over the first mixture and smooth with a spatula. Cool, then cut into squares.

Hot Chocolate

2 litres	whole milk
8 oz	bittersweet chocolate, finely chopped
	marshmallows, for garnish

In a large saucepan, heat the milk. Add the chopped chocolate and stir with a whisk until smooth. Top with marshmallows.

nordic flare...

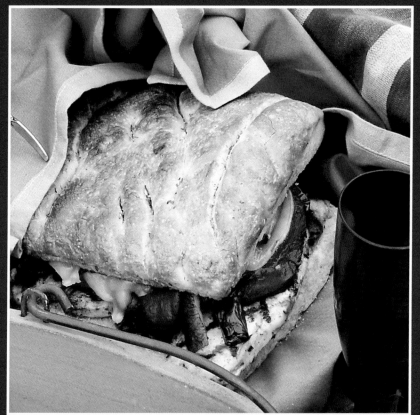

TWICE-BAKED POTATOES

•

GRILLED MEDITERRANEAN PANINI

•

SAUSAGE ON A BUN WITH
CARAMELIZED ONIONS AND PEPPERS

•

DARK CHOCOLATE AND
FRESH ORANGE SEGMENTS

SERVES 8

When crisp snow and bright sunshine are in the forecast, call a friend and wax up your cross country skis. Assemble this make-ahead menu and then have fun and relax, knowing that you will come back to a hearty feast. Round out the meal with your favourite red wine, premium dark chocolate and juicy orange sections.

GETTING ORGANIZED

Up to a day ahead:
Bake and prepare stuffed potatoes.
Grill vegetables and chicken for panini. Assemble panini, and slice onions and peppers.

Final Preparations:
Caramelize onions and peppers on the side burner and grill sausage. Reheat panini and potatoes.

Twice-Baked Potatoes

A great side dish for entertaining, these mitt-warming potatoes can be made several hours or even a day in advance. After filling, cover tightly with plastic wrap and refrigerate. Try a variation with mushrooms and truffle oil or chives.

6	medium baking potatoes, scrubbed and pierced lightly	¾ cup	grated cheddar cheese, plus more for garnish
¼ cup	butter, at room temperature	¼ cup	grated parmesan cheese
½ cup	sour cream, at room temperature	¼ cup	cooked and crumbled bacon, plus more for garnish
¼ cup	buttermilk, at room temperature		freshly ground black pepper, to taste
1 tsp	kosher salt		butter, for dotting the tops
2	scallions, green and white parts, minced		

Preheat oven to 350°F and bake the potatoes directly on the oven rack until tender, about 1- 1¼ hours. Cool 15 minutes.

Laying the potatoes on their sides, cut off the top ¼ and reserve, and gently scoop out the flesh with a spoon, leaving ¼" thick shells.

Force the scooped flesh through a ricer, or mash with a masher in a mixing bowl. Add the remaining ingredients, and gently mix with a fork or a wooden spoon. Taste to adjust the seasonings.

Spoon the filling back into the potato skins, and dot with butter. Replace the cut-off tops and gently wrap with aluminum foil in a way that signals the right-side up. Place on upper rack of a pre-heated barbecue and bake until heated through and beginning to brown, about 30 minutes.

If made ahead and refrigerated, bake for 35-40 minutes.

To serve: Open foil, discard tops and garnish with a little extra grated cheddar and crumbled bacon.

Grilled Mediterranean Panini

This Panini recipe is another example of the versatility of grilled vegetables. For a delicious vegetarian alternative, simply omit the chicken. *See the Vegetable Grilling Guide on page 20* for instructions on how to grill onions, peppers, zucchini and eggplant.

1	loaf focaccia, sliced lengthwise	1	grilled zucchini
½ cup	pesto sauce (recipe follows)	1	grilled eggplant
1	grilled boneless, skinless chicken breast, see Meat Grilling Guide, page 17	1 cup	mozzarella cheese, grated
		1 cup	fontina cheese, grated
1	grilled red onion		olive oil
1	grilled red pepper		

Preheat the barbecue on MEDIUM. Brush the outsides of the focaccia with olive oil and spread the pesto on the cut sides of the focaccia. Layer with slices of grilled chicken breast and grilled vegetables, top with grated cheeses and press the halves together.

This can all be assembled in advance and wrapped in foil until ready to grill.

Place the panini directly on the grids, reduce heat to LOW and cook for 4-5 minutes. Using tongs, turn and cook for another 5 minutes, until focaccia is golden brown and the cheese is melted.

Remove from foil, slice and serve.

Pesto

2 cups	fresh basil leaves, tightly packed		1 tsp	kosher salt
½ cup	olive oil		½ cup	grated Parmesan cheese
2 tbsp	pine nuts, lightly toasted		3 tbsp	unsalted butter, at room temperature
2 cloves	garlic			

Place basil, oil, pine nuts, garlic and salt in the bowl of a food processor and pulse until evenly blended. Turn out into a mixing bowl, and lightly blend in parmesan cheese and softened butter with a spatula.

If using within 7 days, store in a sealed mason jar with a thin layer of olive oil covering the surface of the pesto.

To store up to 6 months, spoon into ice cube trays and freeze. When solid, transfer the cubes to a resealable plastic bag, and thaw as needed.

Sausage on a Bun with Caramelized Onions and Peppers

8	sausages		1	sweet onion, thickly sliced
8	buns			olive oil
1	red pepper, sliced			

Preheat the barbecue on MEDIUM. Toss the onion and peppers with olive oil. Place the sliced vegetables in a cast iron pan over the flame or on the side burner, if you have one. Cook for 5 minutes, stirring often, then reduce heat to LOW, stirring occasionally until onions are softened and brown, about 40 minutes.

Meanwhile, place sausage on the grill. Cook approximately 10-12 minutes per side, until cooked through. During the last few minutes of cooking time, warm the buns on the upper rack.

Dark Chocolate and Fresh Orange Segments

Top quality dark chocolate and some juicy orange sections are a simple but decadent compliment to this outdoor meal.

love potions...

RASPBERRY CHAMPAGNE COCKTAILS

•

BLACK OLIVE CROSTINI

•

GRILLED PEAR SALAD WITH
BLUE CHEESE AND PINE NUTS

•

RACK OF LAMB WITH GREMOLATA

•

WILD MUSHROOM RISOTTO WITH
GRILLED MUSHROOMS

•

STEAMED SUGAR SNAP PEAS

•

CHOCOLATE MOUSSE

SERVES 8

Nothing says love like a home-grilled dinner! This is a delicious dinner party menu which can easily be scaled down for a romantic dinner for two on Valentines Day. Toast the evening with raspberry champagne cocktails and savour appetizers that are effortless to make. Succulent rack of lamb and creamy risotto are balanced by a sweet, crisp salad. As you finish the meal, delight your sweetheart with velvety chocolate mousse.

GETTING ORGANIZED

Up to two days ahead:
Prepare the chocolate mousse, cover tightly and refrigerate.

Up to one day ahead:
Prepare the vinaigrette and toast the pine nuts for the salad, and marinate the lamb.

As the evening unfolds:
Pour the Champagne cocktails, and prepare the gremolata. Grill the crostini and pears. Assemble the salad.
While you are enjoying the appetizers, grill the lamb and mushrooms.
Ask your sweetheart to stir the risotto and steam the peas just before serving.

Raspberry Champagne Cocktails

| 1 | bottle chilled champagne | | fresh raspberries for garnish |
| 1 | bottle Chambourd | | |

Into each champagne flute, pour 3 ounces champagne and 1 ounce Chambourd. Swirl gently to mix and garnish with one raspberry.

Black Olive Crostini

For Valentine's Day we cut the Asiago slices into sweet little heart shapes to set the stage for romance.

| 1 | baguette, sliced into rounds | ½ lb | sliced Asiago cheese |
| 1 | small jar black olive tapenade | | |

On a preheated barbecue set at MEDIUM LOW, grill one side of the bread. Remove from heat and spread the toasted side with black olive tapenade. Top with Asiago cheese and return to grill just until cheese is melted.

Grilled Pear Salad with Blue Cheese and Pine Nuts

3	pears, sliced and peeled	2 tbsp	fresh basil, chopped
1 tsp	olive oil	½ cup	extra virgin olive oil
2 cups	arugula, washed	3 tbsp	balsamic vinegar
6 cups	mixed baby greens, washed	1 tsp	honey
½ cup	pine nuts, toasted	1 tsp	grainy mustard
200 g	semi-soft blue cheese: La Roche, Gorgonzola		salt and pepper, to taste

Preheat barbecue on MEDIUM. Toss sliced pears lightly in olive oil. Place on cooking grids and grill 4 minutes per side, turning carefully.

Prepare salad by tossing arugula and mixed greens in a large bowl.

Toss salad with dressing, prepared by mixing olive oil, balsamic vinegar, honey, grainy mustard, salt and pepper in a bottle and shaking vigorously. Arrange toasted pine nuts, crumbled blue cheese, basil and grilled pear slices on top of tossed greens and serve.

Rack of Lamb with Gremolata

4	racks of lamb, frenched	8 cloves	garlic
8 sprigs	rosemary		zest of two lemons
8 sprigs	thyme	2 tsp	black pepper, freshly ground
10	bay leaves	1 cup	extra virgin olive oil
¼ cup	parsley, chopped		

Marinate the lamb the night before serving. Remove leaves of rosemary and thyme from the stalk and chop with parsley, garlic, bay leaves, lemon zest and pepper. Combine in a bowl with extra virgin olive oil.

Arrange racks of lamb on a large baking sheet, pour on marinade and gently rub into the lamb. Cover with clear plastic wrap and let marinate in the refrigerator overnight. Prepare grids by brushing with oil to prevent sticking half an hour before serving.

Preheat barbecue on MEDIUM for 5-10 minutes. Place racks of lamb on grids and grill for 20 - 25 minutes, following directions for Perfect Grill Marks, page 15. Let stand for 5 minutes, tented with foil, before cutting and serving.

1	lemon	2 cloves	garlic, minced very finely
¼ cup	fresh parsley, finely chopped		black pepper, freshly ground

Finely grate the zest of one lemon. Add parsley and garlic and add a generous grind of black pepper. Serve with lamb.

Wild Mushroom Risotto

5 cups	vegetable stock	2 cups	Arborio rice
2 tbsp	butter	½ cup	white wine
1	medium onion, finely chopped	½ cup	Parmesan cheese, grated
1 clove	garlic, minced	1 tbsp	butter
1 cup	wild mushrooms, chopped		salt and pepper, to taste
2 sprigs	fresh rosemary		

Heat the vegetable stock in a saucepan over medium heat on back-burner.

Meanwhile, melt butter in a heavy saucepan over medium heat, add onion, mushrooms, rosemary and garlic and sauté for 2 minutes.

Mix in rice and continue stirring for one minute. Pour in wine and simmer for 3 minutes, until liquid is absorbed. Add the hot stock, a cup at a time, stirring between each addition, allowing the liquid to be absorbed before continuing with the addition of the next cup of stock. Continue adding stock until rice is al dente and creamy, about 20 minutes. Stir in Parmesan cheese and remaining butter. Top with Grilled Mushrooms.

GRILLED MUSHROOMS:

1 lb	mixed mushrooms, shiitake and cremini, wiped clean and stems trimmed	1 tbsp	fresh rosemary leaves, chopped
			salt and pepper
3 tbsp	olive oil	1 tbsp	balsamic vinegar
1 clove	garlic, minced		

In a flat-bottomed glass dish combine olive oil, garlic, rosemary, salt and pepper. Heat briefly in microwave on HIGH to combine flavours, about 25 seconds. Add mushrooms to the dish and toss to coat. Place mushrooms on a preheated barbecue set on MEDIUM. Turn with tongs until evenly browned and dense in texture. Remove to a serving dish and sprinkle with balsamic vinegar. Use as a garnish for the Wild Mushroom Risotto.

Chocolate Mousse

6 oz	bittersweet (55 %) chocolate, chopped	10 tbsp	butter, softened
4 tbsp	water	⅛ tsp	salt
4	large eggs, separated	2 cups	whipping cream, divided
¾ cup	plus 1 tbsp sugar	1 pint	raspberries
¼ cup	Grand Marnier		

Melt chocolate with water in the top of a double boiler.

Whisk together yolks and ¾ cup sugar in a saucepan over low heat until thickened. Do not allow to boil. Remove from heat and add Grand Marnier.

Beat butter and salt into melted chocolate, then fold the chocolate into the yolks and sugar. Whip 1 cup of whipping cream until set. Fold into chocolate.

With a clean dry bowl, and beaters, whip the egg whites with 1 tablespoon sugar until stiff but not dry. Fold into chocolate mixture. Spoon into individual serving bowls or pretty stemware, and chill well. Whip remainder of whipping cream and spoon over mousse. Top with raspberries.

warm memories...

Mulled Wine

•

Smoked Salmon with
Wasabi Cream Cheese
and Arugula

•

Assorted Olives & Cheese Tray

•

Baked Brie with
Quince Preserves
and Grilled Baguette

•

Green Salad with Oranges
and Manchego Cheese

•

Paella

•

Wendy's Carrot Cake

Serves 8

Your exhilarating day on the slopes does not have to end indoors. Stretch your enjoyment of winter by inviting your guests onto the deck for a warming cup of mulled wine. While they stay cozy under your fleece blankets, fire up your barbecue for a traditional one-dish meal of seafood, chicken, sausage, rice and vegetables. You can do it all on the grill.

Getting Organized

Up to a week in advance:
Bake and freeze the layers for the carrot cake.

Up to one day ahead:
Prepare the Wasabi Cream Cheese, marinate the chicken, make the salad dressing and ice the Carrot Cake.

Before you head out skiing:
Assemble the Brie and Quince, placing it in a tiny cast iron pan if you have one. Put all of the Mulled Wine ingredients except the Vodka in a slow cooker on low so it is ready when you are.
Or just have them all assembled in a saucepan to turn on as soon as you get back.

At the end of the ski day:
Add the Vodka to the strained wine mixture and heat through. Assemble and serve the smoked salmon rolls. With the Brie on the top rack of the barbecue, you can use the rest of the space to grill the baguette slices and then the meat and seafood.
A side burner is a real advantage here, as you can cook the rice for the paella outside at the same time.
When everything is cooked, throw the salad together and you are all set!
Warm up by the barbecue with a cup of hot Mulled Wine while you finish off the menu.

Mulled Wine

1	bottle red wine		2	whole star anise
2	oranges: juice and thick slices of zest		5 pods	cardamom
5	whole cloves		¼ cup	honey
3 sticks	cinnamon		½ cup	vodka

Combine all ingredients except vodka in a saucepan or in a slow cooker until heated through, stirring to dissolve the honey. Strain and add vodka just before serving.

Smoked Salmon with Wasabi Cream Cheese and Arugula

½ lb	smoked salmon, thinly sliced		½ tsp	lemon juice
¼ cup	cream cheese, whipped			salt and pepper, to taste
2 tsp	wasabi paste		1 cup	baby arugula

Combine whipped cream cheese, lemon juice, wasabi paste, salt and pepper in a medium glass bowl.

Lay slices of smoked salmon on a flat surface and gently spread with wasabi cream cheese.

Top with a few leaves of baby arugula and carefully roll up to enclose wasabi cream and arugula leaves.

Cover with plastic wrap and chill for 30 minutes. To serve, stand smoked salmon rolls on end on a simple platter, garnished with a thinly sliced lemon.

Baked Brie with Quince Preserves and Grilled Baguette

1	5 - 6" wheel of brie cheese		1	baguette, sliced
¼ cup	quince preserves			

Line a small cast iron frying pan or other grill friendly vessel with a small round of parchment paper to prevent sticking.

Place the brie in the pan, top it with the quince preserves, and set it on the top rack of a preheated barbecue on MEDIUM/LOW until the cheese is soft and melty, about 10-15 minutes.

Meanwhile, grill the baguette slices until toasted on both sides. To serve, lay the cheese and toasts on a wooden serving platter.

Green Salad with Oranges and Manchego Cheese

8 cups	baby greens		*For the vinaigrette:*	
2	navel oranges, peeled and cut into segments		½ cup	extra virgin olive oil
½ cup	red onion, sliced thinly		2 tbsp	white wine vinegar
½ cup	pine nuts, toasted		1 tbsp	orange juice, freshly squeezed
¼ lb	Manchego cheese, cut into curls with a vegetable peeler		1 tsp	Dijon mustard
			1 tsp	honey
				salt & pepper, to taste

In a large salad bowl combine greens, oranges, onion slices, and pine nuts.

To prepare the vinaigrette: Combine olive oil, wine vinegar, orange juice, Dijon mustard, honey, salt and pepper in a glass jar. Shake vigorously and pour over greens. Toss gently. Top with Manchego cheese curls.

Paella

8	boneless, skinless chicken thighs
¼ cup	olive oil
¼ cup	lemon juice
2 tsp	garlic, minced
2 tsp	spanish paprika
	salt and pepper
1 lb	Chorizo sausage, cut into 8 pieces
½ cup	olive oil
2	small yellow onions, diced
12 cloves	garlic, minced
1	large red pepper, chopped
1	large green pepper, chopped

1 can	28 oz. tomatoes, chopped
3 cups	Calrose rice
4	bay leaves
5 sprigs	thyme, fresh
1 tsp	Spanish paprika
	salt and pepper, to taste
	pinch saffron
5 cups	fish stock
½ cup	white wine
24	mussels, scrubbed
1 cup	green peas, fresh or frozen
24	large shrimp, shelled and deveined
2 tbsp	fresh parsley, minced

Prepare chicken for grilling, by marinating in olive oil, garlic, lemon juice, spanish paprika, salt and pepper.

Preheat grill to MEDIUM and and brush grids with olive oil to prevent sticking. Grill chicken thighs (4 minutes per side) and sausage (10 minutes per side). Set aside and keep warm while rice is being prepared.

Meanwhile, place a large sauté pan directly on top of the grids. Heat olive oil in a sauté pan and add onions and garlic to pan. Sauté 2 minutes, taking care not to brown them. Add green and red peppers and tomatoes, and saute 2 minutes longer. Add rice, bay leaf, thyme, paprika, saffron, salt and pepper, white wine and fish stock. Stir well, bring to a boil and cover. Reduce heat to LOW, close cover and let cook gently for 20 minutes.

Place chicken thighs, sausage, mussels and peas on top of rice, cover pan and cook for 7 minutes over low heat until mussels are open. Meanwhile, place shrimp on grids around the pan and grill 2 minutes per side. Place shrimp on top of Paella and garnish with chopped parsley.

Wendy's Carrot Cake

2 cups	sugar		3 cups	shredded carrots
2 cups	unbleached flour		*For the Icing:*	
2 tsp	baking soda		8 oz	cream cheese, at room temperature
	pinch salt		½ cup	butter, at room temperature
2 tsp	cinnamon		1 lb	icing sugar
1 ¼ cups	vegetable oil		1 tsp	vanilla
4	whole eggs		1 tsp	orange juice
2 tsp	vanilla			

Preheat oven to 350°F. Grease 2 - 9" layer cake tins, and line them with parchment paper.

In a large bowl, mix together sugar, flour, baking soda, salt and cinnamon. In a smaller bowl beat together vegetable oil, eggs and vanilla. Add the wet ingredients to the flour mixture, and combine without over-mixing. Fold in the shredded carrots. Scrape batter into prepared pans, and bake 35-45 minutes on the middle rack of your oven until set or until a toothpick comes out clean.

Let cool 10 minutes before inverting onto cooling racks. Peel off the parchment paper.

To prepare the icing, blend together the cream cheese and butter. Slowly add the sugar, vanilla and orange juice. When cake is completely cool, ice the top of the first layer, then place the second layer over it and ice cake evenly.

If desired, reserve a small amount of icing, tint it with orange food colouring and pipe it decoratively to look like baby carrots around the edge of the cake. Press the blade of a knife lightly and randomly along the "carrots" for a more realistic appearance. You can also tint some of the icing green to look like carrot tops.

Recipe Menu

Index

Metric Conversion

WEIGHT	
½ ounce	15 g
1 ounce	28 g
4 ounces (¼ pound)	112 g
8 ounces (½ pound)	225 g
16 ounces (1 pound)	450 g
1¼ pounds	560 g
1½ pounds	675 g
2¼ pounds	1000 g (1 kg)

MEASUREMENT	
⅛ teaspoon	0.5 ml
¼ teaspoon	1 ml
½ teaspoon	2 ml
1 teaspoon	5 ml
1 tablespoon	15 ml
2 tablespoons	25 ml
¼ cup (2 ounces)	50 ml
⅓ cup (3 ounces)	75 ml
½ cup (4 ounces)	125 ml
⅔ cup (5 ounces)	150 ml
¾ cup (6 ounces)	175 ml
1 cup (8 ounces, ½ pint)	250 ml
2 cups (16 ounces, 1 pint)	500 ml
1 quart	1 litre

TEMPERATURE	
300°F	150°C
325°F	165°C
350°F	180°C
400°F	205°C
450°F	240°C
500°F	260°C
600°F	320°C
750°F	400°C

PUBLISHED BY:
Onward Manufacturing company Ltd.
585 Kumpf Drive, Waterloo, ON CANADA
N2V 1K3

Phone: (519) 885-4540
Toll-Free: (800) 265-2150
Fax: (519) 885-1390

e-mail: info@omcbbq.com
www.omcbbq.com

EDITORS:
Kris Schumacher, Andrea Witzel

FOOD STYLISTS:
Kris Schumacher, Andrea Witzel

PHOTOGRAPHY:
Bryn Gladding

DESIGN AND PRODUCTION:
Bravada Communications Inc.

Printed in Canada by Interglobe Printing Inc.

ISBN 978-0-9811735-0-4
COPYRIGHT © 2009
ONWARD MANUFACTURING COMPANY LIMITED
All rights reserved. First Edition